KIASU KIASI
YOU THINK WHAT?

DAVID LEO

TIMES BOOKS INTERNATIONAL
Singapore • Kuala Lumpur

Illustrations by TRIGG

© 1995 Times Editions Pte Ltd

Published by Times Books International
an imprint of Times Editions Pte Ltd
Times Centre, 1 New Industrial Road
Singapore 1953

Times Subang
Lot 46, Subang Hi-Tech Industrial Park
Batu Tiga, 40000 Shah Alam
Selangor Darul Ehsan, Malaysia

Printed in Singapore

ISBN 981 204 626 7

*For my wife Mary-Anne
and daughters
Cheryl-Jean and Cherie-Nicole*

PREFACE

Allow me to state at the onset that this book does not aim to teach or castigate. If there are hints of castigation, it is incidental and unintended. If the book teaches, well and good. Ultimately, it aims to entertain.

I would also like to pre-empt any wrong perception anyone may have – chancing upon expressions such as *kiasu*, *lah* and *why you so like that!* – that this is a book about *Singlish*. There has already been much debate on Singlish, and it is so easy to be drawn into the inconclusive argument. I can't help but recall a drama course I attended conducted by RTS (Radio & Television Singapore); the trainer/producer insisted that we speak only BBC English. It never quite took off.

At the end of all the debate, I wonder what *Singlish* really is. I take a very simple stand: *Singlish* is not synonymous with bad English and bad English is not necessarily *Singlish*. What's wrong if we call someone a *kiasu*? After all, the English masters adopted many native words whose meanings cannot be fully conveyed otherwise. But if we accept *don't shy, don't shy, join me* and disguise it as *Singlish*, we may end up muttering *don't naughty*, *don't bad* and *don't desperate*.

Some readers may think I am compiling a dictionary or a glossary of Singaporean expressions. I am no lexicographer and do not pretend to be one. But I find that dictionaries have their appeal, because there is a world of discovery between their covers. My book is a dictionary only insofar as it attempts to explain the origin and usage of certain expressions.

I have tried to capture the flavour of how Singaporeans speak and write, to inject in our expressions, or draw from them, as the case may be, some humour. No right or wrong values are attached to these expressions, although the grammatical errors in many of them are quite apparent. There is a section subtitled 'Very Singlish Lah!' and another on 'Singapore Slips', but the intention is not to ridicule or criticise. All said and done, I hope we will pause and, on reflection, enjoy a good laugh at ourselves.

By listening carefully to the things people say, we learn new expressions almost every day. When I started collecting those gems, verbal and written, as some hobbyists collect stamps and matchboxes with a certain passion, I found myself having more fun than I had expected as I analysed them. The reader will find many words and phrases that are expressions influenced by our multicultural heritage, the product of the inevitable intermarriage of our nation's many tongues (dialects included). These I find fascinating. And lest we forget, our manner of speech and the things we say reflect a lot about us as a people of a nation and our values in life.

The reader will discover snippets of Singapore in the sections 'Singapore Slang', 'Made In Singapore' and 'Singapore Lifestyle'. Again, they aim to amuse more than to teach (although the non-Singaporean reader will find much to learn), and certainly not to jibe or offend.

One last word: in case any reader accuses me of making fun of Singaporeans, I must add that I am myself a Singaporean, and proud to be one.

David Leo
June 1995

CONTENTS

The Alphabet & Numbers 13
 1 Let's Begin With The Alphabet
 2 Numbers & Digits

Very Singlish Lah! 17
 3 The Infamous Kiasu
 4 From Kiasu To Kiasi
 5 The Ubiquitous Lah
 6 From Lah To Lor
 7 And Some People Say Meh
 8 You Say What?
 9 Actually, She Says
 10 Then You Know
 11 Not Yet
 12 Got Or Not?
 13 Also Can
 14 So What & So Like That!
 15 On & Off
 16 Yours & Mine: One Too Many
 17 Cars, Buses, Trains & Aeroplanes
 18 Come Follow Me
 19 Come Blow Your Horn
 20 Two Kinds Of Drivers
 21 Treats
 22 Study
 23 Pass Urine
 24 Like Hell, Like Mad
 25 Everything's Okay

26 Want To Doing Something
27 Shoppers & Shopping
28 The Latter Words: After, Wait & Suddenly
29 When She Doesn't Care
30 Last Time, Next Time

Singapore Slang 45
31 Army Days
32 Catch No Ball
33 Shake Legs
34 Go On A Date
35 Strike It Rich
36 Don't Be A Lamp-post
37 Thirteen O'clock
38 Half-past Six
39 The Coffee Shop Is Open
40 Eat The Wind
41 Go Fly A Kite
42 Mountain Tortoise
43 And Other Animals
44 A Three-legged Creature
45 Rice Eater
46 The Fish Is Loco
47 Kelong
48 A-one
49 Fried Or Fired?
50 Eat Rubbish
51 Eat Someone Up
52 No Fish, Prawns Will Do
53 Plain Water
54 What's The Damage?
55 Square Hats

56 Fat Hope
57 That Shiok Feeling
58 Expletives
59 Bogus Lawyers

Made In Singapore 69

60 Made In Singapore
61 Defining Local
62 Acronyms & Abbreviations
63 Names & Buildings
64 More On Buildings
65 The Four Worlds
66 Signs Of The Time
67 Ang Mo Kio
68 King George V Park
69 Things Aquamarine

Singapore Lifestyle 87

70 Greetings
71 Respect For Age
72 Excuse Me, Miss
73 Towkays
74 Hainanese Relations
75 Brothers & Sisters
76 Uncles & Aunties
77 Cousin Brother
78 Ah Huay & Ah Beng
79 Bhai, Chope!
80 Mama, Affectionately
81 Red-haired Devil
82 Peranakan Patois
83 Goo-goo Gaa-gaa

84 Speak Mandarin Campaign
85 Qipao Or Cheongsam?
86 The Polite Civil Servant
87 Police Story
88 Samseng: Ah Seng Or Sam?
89 Distant Cousins & Rhymes
90 Dolly Parton & Chicken Breasts
91 Jumbo For Size
92 The Bald Pate
93 Minding Other People's Business
94 A Staring Incident
95 Face
96 A Ladies' Man
97 Wife Or Lover?
98 Mahjong Players
99 Break A Leg
100 Yamseng!
101 Something To Take Home
102 Heaty Or Cooling Or Windy?
103 Sales
104 Pasar Malam
105 Places Near & Far
106 Wet Market
107 Guaranteed Quality
108 Property Advertisements
109 Have The Cake & Eat It

Cross-Cultural Influences 121
110 A Common Heritage
111 Colours
112 Makan Time
113 Soup & Medicine

114 Milk + Water
115 Eyes See
116 Pleas For Help
117 It's Your Fasal
118 Words That Spell Trouble
119 Death Knell
120 The Hole Of Opportunities
121 Chope Me A Place
122 So Leceh!
123 Tak Pakai
124 Superstitions
125 Go Home
126 A Bump On The Head
127 All's Fair In War & Love
128 Child's Play
129 Kiam Siap & Hum Sap
130 A Tiger In The Bush Or Good Wine Needs No Bush
131 Agak Agak
132 As You Like It

Singapore Slips
and one from across the Causeway 139

133 Boy Or Girl, Make A Guess
134 Second Chance
135 December 25 Is Christmas
136 Heard On Radio
137 Reason In Madness
138 A Time To Kill
139 In Block Capitals
140 The Centre
141 Two Things You Should Not Do
142 First Come First Served

143   Come & Go
144   Play Cheat
145   Neither A Borrower Nor A Lender Be
146   Too Much, Too Little; Too Many, Too Few
147   When It Is Too Much
148   A Matter Of Location
149   A Matter Of Degree
150   Perfection Par Excellence
151   Seeing Double
152   Using The Telephone
153   Hello, Can I Help?
154   Pain Is Painful
155   The Cooker Cooks
156   Win, Lose Or Draw
157   For Whom The Bells Toll
158   No Swimming Allowed

Last Word 157
159   Last Word: Mate

The Author 159

The Alphabet & Numbers

1
LET'S BEGIN WITH THE ALPHABET

There are those among us who don't know that the English language has only one alphabet, and that this one alphabet comprises 26 letters from A to Z. They confuse the alphabet with the letters and refer to the letters as *alphabets*.

Examples of this confusion abound. In a respectable game of chance aired on television, a guest spins some balls in a round receptacle to pick, according to the hostess, three winning *alphabets*. In other game shows, participants are asked to select *alphabets* from A to Z as the correct answers, given the clues. Similarly, in many contests found in newspapers and magazines, readers are asked to match the *alphabets* with scenic pictures or smiling faces.

The *Straits Times* on 22 March 1984 reported the excellent results attained by a college as follows: "The most common *alphabet* in Hwa Chong Junior College today must be A …" Telecoms asked applicants for business telephone lines to "indicate the *alphabet* against which your business/company's registered name would appear in the phone book." And the Public Utilities Board issued a notice to inform consumers that "if your account number contains an *alphabet*, the *alphabet* has been deleted so that you will be able to pay your PUB bills by electronic funds transfer …"

My favourite example is one from an agency promoting an *alphabet play tray* for children: "It helps to improve children's IQ through placing the correct picture into the correct *alphabet* tray, for example, Picture Fish will only fit into *Alphabet F*."

Teach the children well, so they say.

And the clerks at the Passport Office continue to check the *alphabets* of applicants' identity card numbers if these have been omitted. Some superstitious would-be car owners are particular about the *alphabet* in their registration numbers: X is not favoured. And a reputable country club reminds its members to indicate the check *alphabets* of their membership numbers whenever they sign in.

Letter, on the other hand, somehow doesn't seem to convey quite the right connotation: "What's the *letter* of your I/C (identity card) number?" would provoke the retort: "*Letter*? What *letter*? Oh, you mean the *alphabet*."

That letter is, perhaps, best described as the *alpha reference*.

2
NUMBERS & DIGITS

The digits of a number are similar to the letters of the alphabet, in that they are both components of a whole. The digits are in themselves numbers, but they are not *the* number standing alone.

All too often when you have dealings concerning a number comprising several digits, such as a bank account number or a credit card number, you have someone over the counter or at the other end of the telephone line asking, "What are the numbers? Give it to me once again, slowly please." Or, "How many numbers are there? Twelve? But you've given me only eleven; one is missing." Yet, are you really wrong when you reply, "Let me give you the numbers slowly"? Now, are we talking about the numbers as numbers or one specific number of several digits?

That, I suppose, is the problem – when we equate *numbers* with *digits* and use the two words interchangeably. A telephone number is *one* number which, in Singapore, usually comprises seven digits. It does not mean you will then have seven telephone numbers. So it is with the identity card and passport numbers. Thank goodness our house numbers, unlike most American and Canadian numbers, are generally small and easy to remember!

Very Singlish Lah!

3
THE INFAMOUS KIASU

No word, perhaps, is considered more Singaporean than *kiasu*. Literally translated from Hokkien, it means *afraid to lose out*. There is no better way, it seems, to describe the infamous Singaporean trait of not wanting to be second to anyone in anything and everything. Observers are quick to blame the hike in COE and property prices on *kiasuism*.

The original *kiasu* connotation is negative and its usage derogatory. Anyone seen to be *kiasu* invited derision and contempt.

A *kiasu* person can be spotted miles away at a buffet lunch, piling his plate high with food only part of which he is likely to consume. This has prompted many restaurants offering *eat-all-you-can* fare to warn its patrons that they will be charged for food left behind on their plates. A reputable restaurant in a five-star hotel had to withdraw its offer of unlimited orders of any dish from its menu for a flat price, after too many *kiasu* families ordered nothing but abalone, dish after dish. *To get their money's worth lah!*

Mr Kiasu always rushes to be at the head of a queue for anything ranging from free gifts to buying an apartment costing several hundred thousand dollars. He rushes into the lift before the passengers inside can even step out. You might say it has to do with our pace of life: *cannot wait lah!*

In a word, the *kiasu* person is selfish. He always takes more than he needs, even if it means wasting it or depriving others of it. He is inconsiderate. He is greedy. And he is definitely obnoxious.

No wonder some Singaporeans are offended by any suggestion that *kiasuism* is a national trait. It is an ugly tag. Not all Singaporeans, they maintain, behave like that!

Some others reserve a good word for *kiasuism*. Because of his nature, the *kiasu* person will always get what he wants. And he will do a *darn bloody good job* and excel because he always wants to win. And who says it is a sin to want to win? I recall stepping into a queue at a POSBank when a mother quickly pushed her child under the rope of the stanchion to stand a place ahead of me. I was told, when I related the incident to some friends, that the child was likely to succeed in life, having learnt at an early age to quickly seize opportunities as they arose. No amount of classroom teaching can provide the invaluable lesson of a real life experience!

4
FROM KIASU TO KIASI

Some people think being *kiasi* is better than being *kiasu*, because if a person dies, he is wiped off the face of the earth, whereas if he loses, he may still return and win. You've guessed it – *kiasi* is literally *afraid to die* or *dead scared.*

A *kiasi* person is not a fool who rushes in where angels fear to tread. In business he will not want to risk taking on new ventures. He plays safe. People sneer at his timidity and call it cowardice. But maybe he is smart. In a precarious world the slow and cautious have a better chance of surviving the rat race that destroys prematurely too many of the bold and enthusiastic.

5
THE UBIQUITOUS LAH

La, la, la, la, la, la, la, according to a popular song, means "I love you".

There was a time when the use of *lah* (we spell it with the unaspirated *h*) at the end of a sentence was frowned upon as uneducated, lowly and bad English. It is one of those meaningless expressions – not necessarily unemotive – and the most commonly used amongst them, that helps us complete a sentence nicely. But because it sounds so un-English (obviously, since it is not an English habit *lah*), it is considered bad English, and that explains its unpopularity in the past. But society has grown more tolerant, and *lah* is quite often used deliberately in dialogue to reflect the flavour of the local culture. *No use trying to hide our roots lah!*

Foreigners who have stayed long enough in Singapore often try to impress people by dropping a *lah* or two now and then when they speak. I suppose it is part of an acclimatisation programme for living abroad, the same kind of assimilation that has Singaporeans returning from Italy exclaiming *mama mia!* with irrepressible exuberance or from Japan muttering *a-so* earnestly under their breath. One wonders if that makes them in any way more native. Frankly, I don't know *lah!*

6
FROM LAH TO LOR

Lor is as harmless as *lah*, and typically Singaporean. And if *lah* is okay, what's wrong with *lor*?

You hear it almost anywhere.

At school: "He wants to have a copy of the notes, so I give it to him *lor.*"

At work: "Why? Because the boss says so *lor.*"

While shopping: "If you prefer red, take red *lor.*"

Reporting on a date: "She closes her eyes and offers her cheek, so I kiss her *lor.*"

In an aeroplane, a stewardess, when asked what she would do after quitting her job: "Study *lor.*" No, not to be a lawyer but to do her 'A' levels.

The *lor* is really redundant. But some people have the knack of making it sound quite nice. Maybe the English equivalent is *so*, yet it's not quite so.

7
AND SOME PEOPLE SAY MEH

Lah, lor and *meh* belong to the same group of language dressers that we can do without.

Meh – it rhymes with mare – is almost always used in questions: "So many people know and you don't know *meh?*" "Everyone was given a press kit. You don't have one *meh?*" "You're not going to the party *meh?*"

Sometimes it is used to express a doubt or disbelief: "He knows *meh?*" (*I don't believe it!*)

It could well act as the verbal question mark.

If we put *lah, lor* and *meh* together, this is what we get: "He should know I've been trying to avoid him *lah.* But if he insists on buying me expensive gifts, let him (do so) *lor.* I don't care, it's not my problem, as if he doesn't know by now how I feel about him *meh?*"

Some people may be quick to tell me there is a sucker born every minute. But falling in love can be wonderful, even if it means putting up with the *lah, lor* and *meh.*

8
YOU SAY WHAT?

You say what? You go where? You talk to who(m)? You come when? You cry why?

Shortcuts for immediacy, or a lazy manner of speech? This is the Singaporean tendency to turn into a question what appears to have started out unambiguously as a sentence by ending it abruptly with an interrogative: "You want to go where?"

The interrogative object: *Page what?* (in a classroom), *Sing what?* (at a karaoke lounge), *Find what?* (looking for something), *Do what?* (time to kill), *Eat what?* (in a restaurant), *Order what?* (going through the menu), *Win what?* (at a carnival game stall), *Say what?* (dumbfounded on a first date), *Make what?* (watching a sculptor at work), *Read what?* (peering over somebody's shoulder), *Buy what?* (at the supermarket), *Baby number what?* (any number from one onwards), etc.

The interrogative adverb: *Go where?* (at a bus-stop), *Fix when?* (arranging an event or a date), *Pain where?* (attending to an injured child), *Evidence where?* (investigating a case), *Arrive when?* (checking a flight arrival), *Wait where?* (arranging a meeting point), *Sweep where?* (when told to clear some mess), *Post Office where?* ("Don't send me all over the island just to mail a letter!"), *Fire where?* (inquisitive), *On TV when?* (Don't want to miss that programme!), *Do how?* (having lost the instruction manual), *Draw how?* (being no artist), *Go why?* (no reason given when asked to leave), etc.

The interrogative pronoun: *See who(m)?* (at an enquiry booth), *Give who(m)?* (when asked to deliver a parcel), *Friend who?* (reluctant to make peace, pretending there's no such person), *Marry who(m)?* (asks the *kay poh*), *Buy which (one)?* (unsure, too many choices), etc.

9
ACTUALLY, SHE SAYS

Actually must be a pet word among Singaporeans, judging by the frequency of its use. It is like a tic: the involuntary

twitching of the nose, the constant massaging of one eyebrow and the persistent tilting of the head to one side. It has become a habit, one of those words that many of us cannot speak without.

I am amazed at the number of times a friend *actually* uses that word when she narrates what happened at a party she attended reluctantly. She begins and ends with *actually*, punctuating almost every sentence with the familiar word, perhaps for emphasis. It is undeniably a very convincing word.

She says, "*Actually* I didn't want to go to the party, but she persuaded me. It turned out to be quite nice *actually*. There were many people and I didn't expect to see him there *actually*. You know, he wasn't supposed to be present *actually*. She told me he was not going. I must confess, however, that I half expected him to be there *actually*, because they were good friends. Maybe that was why I went *actually*. So what that he went too! It *actually* didn't matter at all. I've got over it, I assure you, the bitterness and the hurt. I *actually* felt quite good about not feeling anything when we met that evening, if you know what I mean. *Actually* it was a kind of relief, that the mess was *actually* over, completely and finally over. I'm feeling very good right now *actually*."

I'm not suggesting that anyone should apologise for over-using that word. I assume it is used not without purpose, as when we say, "*Actually*, this is what happens that evening…"

Habits die hard, we know.

10
THEN YOU KNOW

"I'm telling you not to climb so high. You fall down and break your leg, *then you know*!"

A rather queer expression which may be the literal translation of a Chinese phrase to warn of the possible ominous outcome. It highlights realisation that may come too late, caught between *before you know it* and *then you know it*.

11
NOT YET

The teacher who has yet to arrive is said to *not yet come*. Since the party *not yet finish*, it is rude if we leave. A child waiting to help himself to some goodies on the table will say, when asked if he has eaten, *not yet take* or *not yet eat*. If you're still home when you're expected somewhere else, you *not yet go*. And lunch is not ready because mother *not yet cook*.

Do they sound familiar? I assure you that you haven't heard it all yet. Not yet, not yet, not yet.

12
GOT OR NOT?

There's the mother who admonishes her child: "You got wash or not?" The child who says to her schoolmate, about a book the latter promised to lend her: "Got bring or not?" The supervisor to his workers: "Got do or not?" The concerned hostess to her guests: "Everyone got eat or not?" One participant to another at a competition: "Got win or not?" And a visitor at a fair looking for freebies, to her friend: "They got give free gifts or not?"

That's got to be a favourite expression among many Singaporeans, at home or abroad.

A child, while on vacation in New Zealand, was watching a farmer milk a cow. (Many children who grow up in our concrete jungle have never seen a *real* cow and think that milk comes from the factory or a supermarket.) After a while, the inquisitive little traveller turned to her mother: "Mommy, I cannot see. Got milk come out or not?" The amused farmer, whose square back was blocking her view, turned around and held a pail under her nose, saying proudly, "Got plenty, honey." And the mother was quick to add, "It's milk, darling, not honey."

13
ALSO CAN

The *also can* person is the *no problem* person, accommodating and a natural pleaser.

He can be generous: "I will buy you dinner at the Top of the M. And if you want to go somewhere and dance afterwards, *also can*."

Two very pleasant words, indeed.

But, ladies, this man can be dangerous too on that first date when he cuddles up close and breathes heavily down your neck, muttering, "Why don't we go to my apartment? But if you prefer, your place *also can*."

That is, anything goes. Not just with Barcadi and Coke, as some advertisers may have you believe.

Warning: some users prefer *can also*.

14
SO WHAT & SO LIKE THAT!

This is not the defiant *"So what?"*

The utterer is perhaps best described as one lost for words: *what* is really an adjectival substitute for an attribute he cannot at the moment identify. But everyone seems to understand what he is trying to convey, as when he says, "He's so what, talking bad about me behind my back. This type of people lightning will strike one day!"

There is no need to search for the real word since its *what* surrogate meets the exigency of the moment.

Of course, there is that overwrought, unmistakable, true-blue Singaporean expression, "Why you so like that?" *That*, like *what*, defies description.

15
ON & OFF

On the light. On the switch. On the air-con. On the heater. On the tap. On the kettle. On the washing-machine. On the drier. On the engine. On the TV. On the radio. On the music. And, if the volume is too low, on it louder.

The preposition *on* has become a common Singaporean verb. Quite expectedly, the corollary *off* is also used in the same vein. So it is: Off the light. Off the switch. Off the air-con. Off the heater. Off the tap. Off the kettle. Off the washing-machine. Off the drier. Off the engine. Off the TV. Off the radio. Off the music, but not off it softer.

It looks to me like a matter of convenience. Needless to say, every Singaporean understands the *on/off* instruction and many of them do not seem to mind its lazy form. You can actually tell how long a foreign maid has worked in Singapore when she starts saying things like *on the light* and *off the switch*. The process of assimilation works marvellously well in a Singaporean home.

You must have heard this familiar, clichéd line once too often, when the lights are low and the music is soft, and the players on the silver screen are together alone: "You turn me on when you turn off the lights." Now, imagine one of them saying it under his or her gasping, seductive breath, in Singlish.

16
YOURS & MINE: ONE TOO MANY

This one should be given the *Razzie* award for English as it is spoken in Singapore.

Yours and *mine* have often been substituted by *your one* and *my one*. So also *his* and *hers*, which become *his one* and *her one*. And *theirs* is *their one*. In this case, *one* is not numerical but connotes possession, as in Chinese, where *de* takes the place of the English possessive *'s*. English Language teachers are finding it a difficult task trying to undo this singular obsession with *one*.

The whole island seems strangely infected.

In a playground, one child screams at another: "Hey, this toy is *my one*."

In school, one student says to another: "*Your one* is over there. You cannot use *my one*."

At a food centre, one patron calls out to the vendor, "Fishball *kway teow* with chilli is *my one*."

At the office, a clerk admonishes her colleague, "Don't remove this chair. It is *our boss's one*."

At a department store, two friends compare the goods sold by the same store but at different locations: "The Orchard Road branch *one* is not so good as the Marina branch *one*."

The list goes on.

But the Singaporean's use (or misuse) of *one* is not limited to the possessive case. It is also our brand of the purposeless appendix in the genre of *eh*, *huh* and *oh*, along with the ubiquitous *lah*.

Here are some examples:

When one friend is annoyed with another: "Why are you like that *one*?"

When someone is displeased with the result of a race: "This is no good *one*!"

The next example, which I overheard while riding behind two women and a child on an escalator, takes the cake. Said the mother to her friend who tried to hold on to the protesting child: "He doesn't like to be held *one*. If you try to hold him, he will definitely struggle *one*. And then worse, he will surely fall down *one*. Leave him alone; he's not afraid *one*." The ones simply multiply. Though they never become twos or threes or any other number that is more than one (what else can it be?), it is still one too many!

17
CARS, BUSES, TRAINS & AEROPLANES

Typically Chinese, to travel by any means is to *sit* (in) the vehicle of transportation, be it a car, bus, train or aeroplane. Hence a businessman *sits* car to a meeting with clients, a housewife *sits* taxi to the supermarket, a factory operator *sits* bus to the plant, an office clerk *sits* train to the office, a delivery boy *sits* motorcycle to make his rounds, construction workers *sit* lorry to the work site, some people *sit* boat to cross a river, and children love to *sit* aeroplane when going on a vacation.

If you were not travelling by car, two-wheeler (which presumably takes only the number of seated passengers it is built for) or jet (which allows no standing except in some remote parts of China, India and Africa), you may not actually be able to sit all the way to your destination.

18
COME FOLLOW ME

Situation: A house party has just ended and it is getting late. The guests put their heads together to sort out transportation arrangements since not all of them drive.

A *de facto* leader emerges with a plan:

"Judy and Josie will *follow* Kenneth since the three of you live in Jurong."

"Who wants to *follow* Johnson? Why don't you, Ali?"

"Ken can *tumpang* Simon. Also Ah Goh."

"Sim please give Ranjeet a *lift* to Hougang on your way to Yishun."

"Amy, you *go* in Herbie's car."

"Peter, you *take* Rosie and Molly."

"Angelica, did you say your mother was coming to *fetch* you? Good. Can you also *bring* Linda along, since both of you live in Bukit Timah?"

"Who wants to *ride* with Benny? You, Kim and Tim."

"Steven will *drop* Shirley along the way."

"I will *send* Veronica home."

Needless to say, the host is happy despite some verbal snags: If Judy and Josie were to follow Kenneth, they would not be riding in his car. They would be literally trailing him. Similarly, nobody would want to follow Johnson if it is not to take a lift in his car. *Tumpang* (Malay), *lift*, *go*, *take* (instead of *bring*), *fetch*, *drop* and *ride* (as used in the examples above) are safe. But not *send*.

When you *send* something or someone, you don't go along with it or him or her. You *send* a parcel by post (because you don't have the time or means to take it to its destination yourself). You *send* a letter to a friend (instead of bringing it personally to him). You *send* someone to collect your laundry (because you are not free to do so yourself). You *send* a dog to fetch a stick which you have thrown some distance away (while you sit and wait for the dog to come back with the stick). And you *send* a pestering salesman away with an unforgettable lesson on how to accept "no" for an answer (you don't go with him, of course!)

19
COME BLOW YOUR HORN

Little boy blue, come blow your horn …

But most Singaporeans prefer not to blow their horns when driving; they *horn* instead. "*Horn* him!" screams the backseat driver.

Horn, they should know, is not and cannot be used as a verb.

The *Straits Times* carried an amusing Reuter report on 22 June 1985 about a family of ducks crossing a busy Tokyo highway. Japanese motorists were so tickled by the sight that nobody had the heart to *honk* at them, because they were heading for the Imperial Palace.

The correct word is *honk* and not *horn*.

20
TWO KINDS OF DRIVERS

Some people seem to think that there are only two broad categories of drivers on our roads: the speedster and the road hog.

Portrait of a speedster: impatient, pretentious, grumbles often, swears easily and prone to violence. He suffers from the illusion that he is king of the road. Nickname: *Road Bully*. Likely quote from him: "The road so wide and yet you anyhow drive. If you can't drive, sell your car and take MRT."

Portrait of a road hog: naturally slow, nervous, timid and a pessimist. He suffers from claustrophobia (even out in the open road) and the illusion that the road is always too narrow for too many cars. Nickname: *Slow Coach*. Likely quote from him: "Please don't make me *kan cheong*, or I will surely bang the tree!" (*Kan cheong* is *nervous* in Cantonese).

21
TREATS

We all like treats: to the movies, to a meal or a ride on the carousel. Sweets are treats for the children. And a cruise on the *QE2* would be the ultimate treat for a cruiser.

Somehow a treat usually involves the spending of money: "Let me treat you to tea at the best coffee house in town." The Malays would say, "Let me *belanja* you ..." (That is, "I'll pick up the tab or bill.") *Belanja* means spend, and that's probably how some people get round to saying in English, "Let me *spend* you ..."

I wouldn't want to be spent, would you?

22
STUDY

Remember the anecdote of the misunderstood stewardess

who wanted *to study lor*? Well, Singaporeans are apt to use *study* to mean *pursue studies or a course*, *be in school* or even *a capacity to succeed academically*.

Here is a conversation between two mothers of school-going teenagers:

A: "Your son so young already working, ah?"

B: "What to do? Cannot study so come out and work lor. What about your son?"

A: "See results lah. If he can study, he will continue to study. Maybe he will study until he goes to NS. Study in university is not easy, you know."

B: "I tell you, better study than work. After NS, go university and study some more."

It is definitely an interesting subject worth some study.

23
PASS URINE

One of the first things a child learns at school is asking the teacher for permission to go out and ease himself. And I have heard many a child say, "I want to *urine*."

But can you blame the children when teachers themselves forget that the verb of *urine* is *urinate*? I have also heard teachers conducting classes ask, "Who wants to *urine*?" Children learn fast.

One does not *urine* but urinates or passes urine from the body. Kids sometimes say *pass water* instead. Some parents, when talking to babies and young children, may use *wee* or *wee-wee* while others prefer the localised *shi-shi* which, because of its sibilant sound, acts extremely well as an inducement.

LIKE HELL, LIKE MAD

It's easy enough to understand someone when he complains about the weather being *hot as hell*. We all visualise hell as a burning place.

But when someone works or plays *like hell*, it has nothing to do with the heat of the fire. It is used to express extreme effort (just as hell is supposed to be the ultimate in suffering), though not necessarily with negative connotations.

Interestingly, *like mad* is similarly expressed.

I like this balance: "He works like hell, but when he plays, he plays like mad."

People under pressure will go all the way: "He studies like mad for the examination, or else he'll get hell from his parents."

Meeting deadlines: "We rush like mad!"

A sign of good business: "These items (not necessarily hot cakes) sell like mad."

Strangely, *hell* is an extremely versatile and expressive word:

"There is hell of a lot of food left over at the end of the party."

"He loves her hell of a lot."

"Hell of a sickening day!"

"Let's get the hell out of here!"

"Go to hell!"

Good Heavens! Some people swear with the word too: "What the hell!"

25
EVERYTHING'S OKAY

Singaporeans are inclined to say *okay* (or *all right* or *no problem*) to almost everything, from acknowledging gratitude to salvaging difficult or awkward situations so as to avoid embarrassment or evade unpleasantries.

You thank someone for coming to your party, and he replies, "It's okay." Some others say, "No problem." An Englishman would have said, "It's my pleasure."

You ask a guest whether he likes vanilla or chocolate, and he replies, "It's okay." It can be exasperating.

You thank a neighbour for helping you weed the garden,

and he acknowledges with an "It's all right" when he could have said, "You're welcome."

I heard this one on radio: the host thanked a celebrity for agreeing to an interview on air and she responded, "It's all right."

Somehow *okay* (as with the other two expressions) suggests a certain measure of modesty on the part of the speaker. It is a rather unassuming word, but it can be downright rude if it is delivered with undertones of *no big deal*.

At best, it is vague but safe. Sometimes, I understand, it is difficult to utter the direct *yes* or *no*, so some people prefer the sedate and modest *okay, no problem* or *it's all right.*

But there are times when the simple and humble *okay* is used to assert a contention or dispel a doubt, as when a man tells his suspicious wife: "I came straight home after work, *okay*?" You can tell he has a problem and it's not going to be all right.

26
WANT TO DOING SOMETHING

I received a call from the bank where I maintained a current account, and the voice at the other end of the line informed me I had dated a cheque incorrectly. She would honour the cheque if I "want to coming to the bank" to rectify the error and endorse the correction.

That really got to me! Isn't it easier to say "want to come to the bank"? A member of the public called: "I want to asking you where I can buy airport tax coupons." A supplier:

"I want to asking you when you want the new diaries delivered." The florist: "I want to telling you that we don't have yellow roses."

And just as I thought I had an extreme case of *want to doing something* hiccups, I came home and the maid said she wanted a day off on Sunday because "I want to going shopping, sir."

I want to go to a park and listen to the birds chirp and tweet instead. Birds, I am told, never sing out of tune. Because they don't know how.

27
SHOPPERS & SHOPPING

Singaporeans are great shoppers. Or, shall I say, natural shoppers? Shopping is said to be a national pastime. Not surprising, when Singapore has a national event like *The Great Singapore Sale!*

While there is one group of people who will *want to going shopping* every day of the week, there is another group who will *want to go to shopping* every weekend of the month. We confuse *go to shopping* with *go to a place to shop*. *Shopping* itself is not a place; we can go shopping, but we go to Takashimaya to shop.

***

There is a third group of shoppers who simply gloat over bargains. Here are some excitable ones, four friends whose favourite diversion is sniffing out irresistible, great buys:

First shopper: "Wah lau! So good one ah. Buy one get one free, so must buy."

Second shopper: "I agree with you. Don't buy also cannot."

Third shopper: "Only twenty dollars for this? How come so cheap? Cannot don't buy."

But the fourth shopper is both cautious and suspicious: "Be careful. Got spoiled one or not?"

***

Women form yet another special group of shoppers: they do not generally consider imitation a form of flattery. So complains one shopper to her companion: "Why you so like that? (Or *Why you so funny?*) People buy you also want to buy. No mind of your own. Please don't follow me. Why don't you choose another pattern? No good to wear the same dress. People will make comments."

Many of us seem too bothered about *other people making comments.* The assumption is that other people don't normally have good things to say about us. Often, the advice is:

"You'd better not interfere, or he will surely *say you*." To *say* somebody is to criticise or scold that person. I have heard a staff member pleading on behalf of a colleague who has made a blunder: "Please don't say him!" And in a tussle between pride and discretion, the former always prevails: "You must never let him say you!"

***

Shoppers are apt to make comparisons, as when this woman eyeing a last item picked up by another person says to her friend, "Her that one is nicer. I'm going to grab it if she dumps it."

Who says shopping is non-competitive?

28
THE LATTER WORDS:
AFTER, WAIT & SUDDENLY

This basket of words made up of the conjunction *after*, the verb *wait* and the adverb *suddenly* is a cluster of what I call the *latter* words; they introduce events consequential to an aforementioned subject.

After:
"I must think before I speak when you're around, *after* I make mistakes."

"She doesn't want to go to the party, *after* she gets embarrassed meeting her ex-boyfriend there."

"Don't be late, *after* your mother gets angry."

And, at a magic show, a little boy is heard telling his sister: "*After* got magic come out!"

Wait:

"You spend so much money on that dress, *wait* your mother scolds you."

"He makes so many mistakes, *wait* he gets sacked."

"You ask so many questions, *wait* he thinks you're interested."

Suddenly:

"If I go there, *suddenly* he comes here, we will never be able to meet each other."

The Malays seem to have the perfect substitute: *sekali*, as in this example: "I'd better stay home and wait for him. If I go to his house, *sekali* he comes here." Which came first, *suddenly* or *sekali*?

29
WHEN SHE DOESN'T CARE

Seemingly defiant, when a person utters repeatedly "I don't care!" he seems to be borrowing a line from a pop song that doesn't mean much. Short of being swear words, they are really tantrum words of annoyance and helplessness, uttered to let out steam or vent one's anger.

So what do you do when someone screams, "You broke my vase. I don't care! I don't care!"

I suppose, if you are the cause of the commotion, you care enough. But when *she* doesn't care, you wonder if you should be bothered at all!

Yet, don't be mistaken. Hers is not really the *tidak apa* attitude of some people: those who are either disinterested, indifferent or couldn't care less. On the contrary, she cares enough to be screaming her head off; those others would not bat an eyelid as nothing upsets or ruffles them. The best historical example must be the Roman emperor, Nero, who fiddled away while Rome burnt.

30
LAST TIME, NEXT TIME

Children are apt to say, understandably, *last time*, when referring to the past: "*Last time* my mother took me to school in her car, but now I go on my own by bus." And when they grow older, they may not be able to kick the habit: "*Last time*, when we were children, we used to go to the park to play." Many people are quick to point out that all of us were children only once.

Not too long ago, a local film critic in a TCS interview on Channel 5 said that new film productions were "not like movies *last time*". Another case of habits dying hard, indeed!

If there were a *last time*, is there a *next time*? Can you doubt it? "*Next time* when I grow up, I want to be a pilot."

Singapore Slang

31
ARMY DAYS

Army boys have developed a jargon of their own. Because Hokkien is commonly used, some Hokkien terms have been anglicised, the most popularly used of which is probably *kooning*, or *sleeping*, as in *caught kooning*. (*Koon*, as you have probably guessed, is *sleep*.) So an army boy who sleeps a lot is crowned a *koon king*.

There is, of course, *jia chua* (literally *eat snake*), the equivalent of skive. It is popular not only in army camps but also at the office. Some people have used *snake* (as a verb) to mean the same thing – probably because the snake is known to be a creature that sleeps aplenty. The word should not be confused with *sneak*. But *snake* used as a noun has its usual biblical meaning: someone you should be wary of; cunning, sly and slimy, one likely to betray your trust.

The *snake* (verb) synonyms include *ponteng* and *play truant*, familiar words we pick up in school. I grew up with the notion that it was a French trait, hence the expression *take French leave*. And when we start working, this mis-demeanour is better known by a less charming but more businesslike straight-to-the-point term: AWOL, or Absent Without Leave.

The *koon king* has a relative: the *tolak king*. (*Tolak* is Malay for push or put aside.) Such a person is a shirker of responsibility. And if he goes on frequent medical leave, he earns the honours of an *MC king*, better known to his employer as a malingerer. (*MC* is short for medical chit or certificate.)

Blur also features popularly in army lingo, so a *blur king* is one who is always confused and lost. He has an equally

ITS KOON KING KING KONG!

TRIGG

befuddled companion: the *gabra king,* who is so nervous that he cannot think straight.

The regal line-up includes yet another kind of king – the *sabo king* who is an expert at playing people out. The root word of *sabo* is, of course, *sabotage.* You might warn such a person: "Don't you dare *sabo* me!"

Interestingly, the operator of a food outlet in Marine Parade claims uncertified honours as the nation's "Sabo King" because he dishes out a variety of rice and noodles cooked in claypots. *Sabo,* in this case, has nothing to do with sabotage; it is Cantonese for claypot. That confuses matters and leaves the interpretation field open for the search of the true blue *sabo king.*

As I venture to introduce another very popular army word, I must first beg the ladies' pardon. My wife objects vehemently because it is vulgar, an expression I myself do not encourage. But it is often heard in the company of men, as when my boss looks around surreptitiously to make sure there are no women present before he shoots off a *cock-up* remark when things foul up. There are exceptions. A woman in my company had all the men agog when she screamed, "Don't talk cock!" I beg your pardon, indeed.

32
CATCH NO BALL

This seemingly vulgar expression – *catch no ball* – swept through the eighties like a tidal wave. Its popular usage in the army, on TV and out in the streets was an infectious streak.

Its origin is Hokkien. If someone *catches no ball*, he simply does not understand. The inability to grasp the meaning of something said or done is like the inability to catch a ball. But to play *real* ball, sports experts emphasise the prerequisite of possessing ball sense, and unfortunately not many people qualify. To be able to catch a ball is not as easy as it appears.

33
SHAKE LEGS

When an Englishman says he is *twiddling his thumbs*, not many Singaporeans understand him. And when a Singaporean announces that he is *shaking legs* at home, the Englishman is baffled. Different parts of the body, but surprisingly they do the same job. Idiomatically, I mean.

The Englishman is probably more nimble and demonstrative with his thumbs, but the Singaporean finds it easier to shake his lower limbs. The former idles playing his thumbs, and the latter bides his time with some visible leg movements. Neither is in any hurry.

There is another interesting expression, which probably originated in a time when houseflies proliferated. So people who got laid off or who stopped working were often said to be staying home to *swat flies* – something we would not normally do unless we had the time. With many public campaigns and relentless efforts to rid our nation's grounds of these and other pests, fly swatters might well be a dying breed themselves!

34
GO ON A DATE

To go on a date, that is, to go out with someone of the opposite sex, is to *patoh*. Somehow any suggestion by a third party of such an intention usually causes the involved parties to blush. There are obvious hints of intimacy.

It is, however, not an activity confined to young, unmarried couples earnest about developing a love relationship. Older, married couples may find the excuse to *patoh* when their grown-up children invite their friends or dates home, just to be out of their way!

35
STRIKE IT RICH

Many Singaporeans dream of *touching* (that most intimate of all senses) lottery in games of chance such as 4-D and Toto which offer huge monetary prizes.

The Chinese word is *zhong*, and it is a wonder how it becomes *touch* in English. It is probably the act of coming into contact – to lay hands on big sums of money – more aptly described as *hit* or *strike* (the jackpot). So it is hitting the first prize or the jackpot, or striking lottery as in striking gold or, in this age of scarce energy sources, oil.

The Malay equivalent is *kena*.

While to *kena* a lottery is a one in a million chance, it is not so remote a possibility that an ill-mannered child will *kena* scolding from his mother; that a stubborn pupil at school will *kena* punished by his teacher; that a lazy worker will *kena* sacked by his employer; that if you're not careful when you bathe, soap can *kena* your eyes; and that a thief, no matter how smart, will one day *kena* jailed by the law.

36
DON'T BE A LAMP-POST

Can you beat it! SBC (now TCS) had it in a subtitle for a Chinese drama as *play gooseberry*. Nothing wrong with it: it's perfect English but perhaps, pardon me, much too English.

Alas! The local viewer would have understood it better had it been *don't be a lamp-post*. The third person is a *lampu* (Malay for *lamp*), something that courting couples and lovers don't need. So the brighter the *lamp*, the more inconsiderate or interfering he or she is said to be.

In an awkward situation like this, a new usage of a familiar word has evolved as a life-saver: the courting couple wish that the third person would be *automatic* (i.e., have the initiative, act without being told) and leave them alone.

37
THIRTEEN O'CLOCK

This time-based expression, whose origin is Chinese, is derogatory and refers to someone who is off his rocker, harebrained or scatterbrained. It reminds me of the female protagonist in the early Goldie Hawn movies.

Twelve o'clock is as far as you can go on a traditional clock. Thirteen o'clock is, therefore, something not quite right, like a pendulum that has swung beyond its limits. Maybe we should re-examine its usage since the time of the day is divided into twenty-four hours and the thirteenth hour has gained international acceptance as one hour past noon.

Some clocks go *ding dong*, which incidentally rhymes with *ting tong*, another Chinese expression for a crazy person.

38
HALF-PAST SIX

Half-past six is the time that the boss complains about shoddy work or work half-done. I have tried in vain to figure out how this expression describing deplorable results came about, fixing my mind's eye on the straight line formed by the hour and the minute hands on the face of a clock. However derived, one thing is clear: the workers will have to pull up their socks and stop watching the clock.

39
THE COFFEE SHOP IS OPEN

Little children are such fun to listen to. A little girl carelessly reveals her underwear when she sits on a chair, legs apart.

Her playmates jeer, chanting, "Shame, shame, open coffee shop!"

40
EAT THE WIND

The English have always considered the wind elusive and wayward, and they speak ill of the north wind that blows nobody any good. The Chinese and the Malays alike *eat the wind* when they go on a holiday: *chifeng* (Chinese) or *makan angin* (Malay). Perhaps it has to do with the freedom or carefree nature of the wind. Going on a vacation really means leaving all your cares behind and doing nothing but breathe in the air – presumably there are still places in the world where the air is fresh and clean.

But too much wind can be bad for one's mental health. If it gets into a person's head, he becomes crazy, bringing on a case of *tou feng* (literally, *head wind*). In the same way, it is bad too if wind has gone into the stomach, as happens to babies, who have to be burped after each milk feed. So you may ask, why *eat the wind* then?

41
GO FLY A KITE

The *Straits Times* of 24 June 1994 reported that a Princeton graduate lecturer at a polytechnic flew a kite and cut fruit to teach calculus to her students. Unfortunately the report did not say how but quoted the astrophysics major as saying, "I think the sight of their lecturer running around with a kite was too much for them."

Although kite flying is a popular activity in Singapore, the expression *go fly a kite* (like its cousin *go jump in the lake*) is not Singaporean as some people I know seem to think. It's an unsubtle hint that someone is *persona non grata*. But I am told it has a more sinister meaning, which is offensive and definitely local: the insinuation that a man should retreat into the bush to do his own thing!

42
MOUNTAIN TORTOISE

That's *suaku* in Hokkien, somebody so uncivilised that he does stupid or embarrassing things. *Primitive* aptly describes him, and so does *country bumpkin*. In the old days, the word was *sinkeh* (new guest), meaning a new immigrant from China, a label inviting derision.

43
AND OTHER ANIMALS

The other woman is not a popular figure. She has been typecast as a home wrecker, a woman of loose morals, a cheap sort, a slut, a harlot and one who steals another woman's husband. The Chinese call her a *vixen*, not necessarily the bad-tempered quarrelsome woman as defined by the *Oxford Advanced Learner's Dictionary of Current English.* That, to the Chinese, is more likely the *tigress.*

Then there is the *boaster cock* or someone who is very *yaya* (Malay). Probably because the rooster is a bird that not only takes pride in its crowing but also struts about unabashedly showing off its beautiful plume.

Just as unpopular is the *crocodile* or *buaya* (Malay) for men. In golf, the *buaya* cheats on his handicap and preys on honest players. Outside golf, his motives are suspect when he befriends women.

And this last one baffles me: why is someone who acts silly often said to have *no cow sense*?

44
A THREE-LEGGED CREATURE

This creature of the homo sapiens species has three legs and is not really a freak. He is a common sight in the concrete jungle of office buildings where he engages tirelessly and shamelessly in office politics. Naturally he is unpopular among his colleagues who scorn him for his demeaning behaviour. He *saka* the boss, they say. He is therefore the boss's third leg – his *fetch-and-carry man*, the runner or the gopher. I suspect that this three-legged creature in question uses his third leg to support his object of admiration, if not to help him walk faster.

Saka (Hokkien) is literally *three legs* or *three-legged*, and *to saka somebody* is to serve as his third leg.

The English idiom is *curry favour*, an interesting term since Singaporeans generally are fond of curry. But, according to the *Oxford Advanced Learner's Dictionary*, to *curry* is to "rub down and clean (a horse) with a curry-comb". Maybe what works is that soothing feeling brought on by the massage.

Commonly used in the same genre of *three legs* is the familiar *tripod* which, of course, provides excellent support.

Other more popularly used terms include *carry* and *angkat* (Malay). Both words imply some form of support being rendered. *Carry* on its own is actually only half of a vulgar expression (*carry balls*) which requires no explanation – now that really hits below the belt and where it hurts most. It beats grovelling on the floor and kissing or licking boots, similar activities conducted way below the belt.

45
RICE EATER

For young women, there are sugar daddies. For older women, there are toy boys. And for rich women, there are men who will eat rice off their slippers.

It is a Cantonese idiom, *eating slipper's rice*, and a loathsome thing for a man to do. In the West, the same man probably drinks champagne from his keeper's glass slipper.

But one who eats a lot of rice is a *fan tong*, literally a *rice barrel*. That does not make him a wiser man than one who has consumed more salt than rice, as an older Chinese man is apt to tell a younger fellow, "Don't teach me old tricks; I've eaten more salt than you've eaten rice."

46
THE FISH IS LOCO

Only a Singaporean will understand what it means when a fish is said to be *loco*. Of course, the fishmonger is unlikely to admit that a fish he sells may be *loco* – and I always wonder how anyone can tell if it is until he eats it – just as a flower girl will always claim that her blossoms are the most fragrant of the season.

Some people define *loco* as stubborn, hence a *loco* fish is one whose meat is tough.

STALLONE TROUT AUNTIE VERY TOUGH ...—

In Hainanese, *loco* is stupid; the more commonly known word to the other dialect groups in the Chinese community is *bonggang*, which is offensive. I would think it a great insult to call someone a stupid fish, *loco* or not, although fish do not normally look that stupid in water. The *loco* fish must be an exception. Let's face it: there will always be the odd fellow in a school. And even the smartest buyer of fish at the market cannot spot that rare bird of a fish. Speaking of birds, in India the *Bombay duck* is really a fish. And in Singapore, an expensive and exotic dish known as *geoduck* served by some Chinese restaurants is really a kind of sea animal harvested off the western coast of North America.

47
KELONG

Soccer or football is easily one of the most popular sports among Singaporeans, more so as a spectator event.

Soccer fever reaches its highest pitch during the World Cup and the Premier League/Malaysia Cup tournaments; the World Cup matches are telecast live over TV and until 1994 the Premier League/Malaysia Cup games were played either in Singapore at the Kallang Stadium or in Malaysian towns.

The *Lions* (so named for obvious reasons) make up the Singapore team, and the thundering support rising from the stadium ground is the unmistakable, 20,000 to 60,000-strong *Kallang Roar*.

A new term that has crept into Singapore soccer lingo is *kelong*, used to accuse a player of accepting a bribe and faking play. The *New Paper* (1 August 1994) reported that "A number of leading soccer players were questioned by

anti-corruption officers as part of a major investigation over the weekend … The CPIB [Corrupt Practices Investigation Bureau] action comes amid constant talk of *kelong* or match-fixing …"

The *New Paper* again headlined a story "KELONG" on 2 September 1994, reporting that six Malaysian journalists were helping in a match-fixing probe. In a box story, the poser was: "Why *kelong* talk now?" One team manager was indignant that players who had known of the corruption did not report to the police then but were "making press statements now".

The *Straits Times* on 5 September followed up with an interview with national footballer and captain, Fandi Ahmad: "*Kelong* is selling out the country, says Fandi." And in a feature story on 20 September 1994, the *New Paper* quoted an ex-national footballer as saying, "You don't have to *kelong* to drive a BMW or have money in the bank." He became a millionaire investing in real estate.

I asked a number of people how *kelong*, a Malay word for a structure constructed out at sea to trap fish, has come to mean someone on the take. They explained how water flowed between the sticks holding up the structure, directing fish into the trap or net (this clue is incidental). I thought of the ball rolling as smoothly into the goal mouth between the poles. But with the *kelong*, it all happens under water and is therefore never above board!

48
A-ONE

It is easy enough to understand that *A-one* means the very best.

The fishmonger at a wet market in Marine Parade that I patronise reserves the best fish for his regular customers. I am one of those privileged to be given the choicest selection which he deftly hides behind him while the general crowd take their pick of the open spread. And each time he holds up a white pomfret to let me see, he proclaims proudly, "A-one!" I just have to believe him.

49
FRIED OR FIRED?

The Cantonese have an interesting expression: *chao yao yi*. Now, is that *fried* or *fired*?

Literally translated, *chao* is fry and *yao yi* is squid. Incidentally, it is a popular dish in seafood restaurants. The squid is prepared in oil over a big fire to the degree that it looks pitiably charred when it is served, sometimes with a dash of lime for amelioration. And that is *fried*.

But when someone is given the boot, that is *fired*. Not exactly a case of leaping from the frying pan into the fire; it's bad enough in the pan!

50
EAT RUBBISH

I have always found this expression strange: "Let's buy some rubbish to eat." How can anyone ever eat *rubbish* and enjoy it? But it seems many Singaporeans do.

Rubbish, the edible sort, refers to a variety of tidbits such as sweets, *kanas* (preserved olives), peanuts, cuttlefish and dried fruit that you can find at a supermarket or a *mama* stall (for *mama*, see #80). While we usually give ugly things beautiful names – the Chinese have a knack for doing this, as when chicken feet are served as *phoenix claws* – *rubbish* seems a most inappropriate term to describe those treats to the palate. Could the reason be that those tidbits are really superfluous to our diet, food we could do without and yet not feel starved or in any way nutritionally deficient? Or that some of the items sold at the *mama* stall are converted from things that would otherwise have ended in the trash bin, such as orange peel and mango skin?

The more plausible explanation is best drawn from a mother's admonition to her child not to eat *rubbish* as it will destroy the appetite for the nutritional food served at regular mealtimes.

51
EAT SOMEONE UP

I asked a young bouncer at a discotheque whether anyone he had thrown out had returned to settle old scores with him.

"That depends," he said, "on whether they think you are easy to *makan* or not."

In its literal sense, *makan* is Malay for *eat*. To *makan* someone is to bully, intimidate or take advantage of him. In English, it is common enough to hear of someone eating somebody alive or eating him for breakfast. But in the cult language of the underground or of certain small, closed circles, to *eat* somebody carries sexual undertones.

52
NO FISH, PRAWNS WILL DO

Still on the subject of food, this interesting Chinese expression advises those who can't get fish to settle for prawns, going down the priority list for the next best option. An Englishman may remind us that beggars do not have a choice.

53
PLAIN WATER

In our sweltering climate, Singaporeans are fond of water as plain as it can be when they get tired of tea and coffee. Yet how plain can water be when someone asks for a glass of not just water but *plain water*? Worse, a plain glass of water.

Sometimes we are over-cautious about the ever-present possibility of misinterpretation where the spoken word is concerned, hence we labour at making ourselves as plain

(I mean, clear) as can be. Of course, *plain water* means just water, not Coke or some syrupy concoction.

I recall travelling with a colleague in Zurich. We stopped at a restaurant for lunch and the waiter asked what drinks we would like to go with our meal. My colleague asked for water (he didn't ask for plain water).

The astonished waiter suggested, "Mineral water?"

"No, just water," said my colleague and, noticing the puzzled but not too friendly look on the waiter's face, went on to ask, "Is there anything wrong with the water coming from the tap in Switzerland?"

I suppose a waiter in a restaurant in Singapore might well ask my colleague, just to be sure, "You mean *plain* water?" Anyway, my colleague got what he wanted: water as plain as it could be.

A word of caution though, as water running from the taps in some countries, plain or otherwise, may not be potable.

54
WHAT'S THE DAMAGE?

Going Dutch is an acceptable social practice with Singaporeans. So if you foot the bill on behalf of a group of people, they are likely to ask you at the end of the celebration, "What's the damage?" If they don't, tell them what the *damage* amounts to, unless you intend to give them all a treat.

In the same manner, if you have to contribute towards a gift for a friend on some joyous occasion like a wedding or the birth of a child, don't forget to ask, "What's the damage?" And, having asked, please do pay up promptly.

WHAT'S THE DAMAGE?

DEPENDS IF YOU'RE THE TITANIC OR THE ICE BERG...

BILL

It's the typical Singaporean way of saying, "What's my share?" Or, "How much do I have to pay?" And *damage* probably best explains the dent it is making to one's pocket or purse!

55
SQUARE HATS

Young graduates in their first job may find themselves enmeshed in the web of experience vs qualifications. Those without similar qualifications but who have spent donkey's years in the same job may resent the entry of academically better qualified men whom they are quick to dismiss as *square hats*.

The expression has nothing to do with the shape of the graduates' heads but alludes to the mortar boards they wear at convocation. I don't think there is any insinuation of the *square hats* being square pegs in round holes.

These days, with even five-year-old kids moving out of kindergartens donning the square hats, sentiments have changed. There are just too many of them entering the job market every year.

56
FAT HOPE

Fat hope seems to mean just the opposite of what it suggests. It is illusory, a desire unlikely to be fulfilled. The Chinese equivalent in Hokkien is *tan ku* (wait forever) and the Malay, perhaps a little less onerous, *sampai tua* (wait until old).

If hope is not *fat*, then there is very little left to hope for. The Chinese generally prefer *fat* to *lean* in most things, as fat symbolises fulfilment and is a sign of prosperity but lean suggests starvation. Nothing like a fat *hongbao*!

However, the preference is not just Chinese, if you will recall the wise words of Caesar:

"Let me have men about me that are fat;

Sleek-headed men, and such as sleep o' nights:

Yond Cassius has a lean and hungry look;

He thinks too much: such men are dangerous."

—Shakespeare, *Julius Caesar*

If hope is fat, ambition is lean and mean.

57
THAT SHIOK FEELING

That *shiok* feeling is more than just a good feeling. It is, as some people might say, *damned good* or *darn good*. It is the best kind of pleasurable feeling that you can get.

The range is tremendous, from biting on red-hot chillies to riding a rollercoaster. It verges on the peaks of pleasure. Even if the chillies burn your tongue. Even if the rollercoaster is spine-chilling and scares you witless. No doubt about it, *shiok* is ecstasy.

58
EXPLETIVES

Alongside the imported *Oh, God! My God! Jesus Christ!* and *Good Heavens!* is the unmistakable *Alamak!* of Malay origin. It is amazing how universally we always look up when we want to scream our heads off! My ex-boss, a devout Christian, thinks that such expressions are blasphemous and exclaims instead, "My word!" and "Godfathers!" Others turn to the animals: "Holy cow!" and "Holy mackerel!"

Other expressions such as *Shit!* are not quite as pleasant. And I don't really know how *Basket!* became a swear word among schoolboys to replace the stronger and forbidden *Bastard!* In the same family are *Idiot!* and *Bloody fool!*

Impressionable teenagers, influenced by American movies, usually live through phases of experimental vogue language. In the early eighties, they were pointing fingers at *nerds*. The local equivalent is *sotong* – squid.

Army boys, finding another marine euphemism for that unmentionable, censored four-letter word, scream profanity: "What a fish!" When you hear it, try pretending it is the long-suffering mackerel!

59
BOGUS LAWYERS

The *Straits Times* of 15 March 1995 carried the story of how a bogus lawyer charged an insurance manager $13,000 in legal fees after advising him to plead guilty to a charge of molest, apparently so that he would get away with only a fine. The sentence turned out to be stiffer than expected: eight months' jail and three strokes of the cane.

Alas, there are all too often too many people who are more than ready to offer advice, whether invited or not, and whether out of goodness of heart or mere nosiness or, as in the case reported, with the intention to exploit a victim's vulnerability for pecuniary gain. In our multilingual society, good and truly qualified lawyers are much respected, not to mention among the nation's top income earners. Those others who profess to be what they are not or who think they can offer good, unqualified advice that may harm more than help are better known as *lawyer buruk*, more like the empty vessels that make the most noise. (*Buruk*, a Malay word that literally means ugly, in this context refers to something old, of no use, and hence dispensable.)

Made In Singapore

60
MADE IN SINGAPORE

(1) Things Instant

Instant trees are a Singapore phenomenon. An expatriate consultant who was involved with the planning and construction of Singapore Changi Airport was impressed by how very quickly the government authorities put in mature trees even before the airport took shape. Those *instant trees* have achieved fame within the region with some of our neighbours showing an interest to grow them.

Things instant have indeed made life that much easier: *instant coffee* and *instant tea* for that quick gulp before you catch the MRT to work, *instant milk* without having to stir the powder for hours, *instant porridge* for days when the wife is away on vacation or the maid has taken off, and *instant lucky draw prizes* as soon as you draw a number from a box without having to wait for months for results to be published in some obscure corner of a cluttered newspaper page.

And, situated at the crossroads of many cultures, it is not surprising that advertising consultants have suggested Singapore as a showcase of *Instant Asia*. After all, Walt Disney successfully created an *instant* world at Epcot Centre.

(2) Marathons

There was a time (and there still is) when every event was an offshoot of the marathon: walkathon, jogathon, cyclathon, etc. The *thons* assume the stature of grandeur, events organised on the largest scale ever.

(3) Mass Weddings

Then there is the fashion to do things en masse, and mass weddings are promoted to save costs and cut down the hassle of handling the details yourself as you leave them to an agency. The concept is gimmicky and has impact, as a picture of 500 brides in tow always makes an interesting story for the Sunday papers. But what about the romance of that day being special for only you?

Mass production is often seen as a cheap manufacturing process. Management gurus are quick to redefine it as mass customisation to satisfy some yearnings for individuality. On a morbid note, don't we always feel kind of sad when we read about mass burials of unidentified victims of war?

(4) Manias

When I was a teenager, *Beatlemania* swept across the young world like a tidal wave. Recently, Orchard Hotel invited its patrons to a *shockamania* lucky draw!

61
DEFINING LOCAL

A friend was quite hung up about the purportedly incorrect usage of the word *local*.

We were having lunch at a coffee-house in a reputable hotel in the tourist belt of Orchard Road. The menu served up both international and *local* fare. My learned friend maintained that Hainanese chicken rice, prawn noodles, wanton mee, mee goreng, laksa, tahu goreng, gado gado, nasi biryani, etc, were not *local* but Singaporean food.

He lamented the loose use of the word *local* by Singaporeans, to mean Singaporean. For example, local beer such as Tiger and Anchor as opposed to imported brands such as Heineken, Carlsberg and Tsingtao. And Singaporeans identify themselves as *we locals* as opposed to foreigners. Alas, it is so widely used as such that it has been accepted to mean just that. Politicians use it, appealing to the *local* community for support. So too the university dons who discuss the limited works of *local* writers and who persuade the government to assist *local* companies that want to venture overseas. And the broking houses monitor closely the volatile performance of the *local* bourse.

HOW DO YOU DO?
I'M A LOCAL
FOREIGNER

According to A.S. Hornby's *Oxford Advanced Learner's Dictionary of Current English*, *local* describes a subject belonging to a particular place or district. The lexicographer provides this example: "Following the national news we have the *local* news and weather." I can imagine my learned friend at lunch arguing that *local* news in Singapore is really national news, so is the weather. By his definition, nothing is really *local*, unless we can discover a tree that is indigenous to Toa Payoh or talk about the weather typical of Changi. Conversely, everything *local* must be national.

What's the fuss really? The word has served its purpose and continues to serve us well. We all understand the telephone bill we receive from Telecoms, showing the charges for *local* and overseas calls. We all know what to expect when a restaurant serves only *local* food. And, of course, *local* time is really only one time for Singapore when we deal with people from around the world. There is no need for us to apologise for our nation's small land size.

I was quite amused when Miss Singapore introduced herself at the Miss Universe Beauty Pageant as coming from Telok Blangah, Singapore. The other participants before her had proudly announced places like Auckland, New Zealand; Sydney, Australia; London, England; Sao Paulo, Brazil; Mexico City, Mexico; New Delhi, India; Tokyo, Japan; and Tel Aviv, Israel. Can you blame her?

I had a similar experience while attending an executive management programme in the USA. The participants were largely American, coming from cities such as Chicago, Illinois; San Francisco, California; Portland, Oregon; Salt Lake City, Utah; Atlanta, Georgia; Miami, Florida; Dallas, Texas; and Boston, Massachusetts. There were only a handful of foreigners from countries the Americans had no problem recognising: England, Switzerland, Japan, Saudi Arabia and the Philippines. When I introduced myself as from Singapore, I saw puzzled looks. One of them asked me, "Which state?"

And it was not surprising when, as my wife signed in at a Las Vegas hotel, the receptionist added *China* on her card, after *Singapore*. The *National Geographic* had in one of its issues lamented Americans' poor knowledge of geography. A lawyer from a big organisation in Memphis sent me a letter addressed to *Singapore, China*. When I finally met the lawyer and his wife in Singapore, I had to settle a dispute between them. According to the husband, Singapore was south of Japan. The wife maintained it was east of the Suez

Canal. You can't fault either, can you? Vandal Michael Fay might have helped place Singapore on the American world map, though I would not be too surprised if many people in Dayton, Ohio got it mixed up the way my lawyer business associate and his wife did.

My learned friend rightly used the USA as an example to explain the real meaning of *local*. A murder in Dayton, Ohio would be considered *local* news. But the caning of a *local* boy charged with acts of vandalism in faraway Singapore was national news. Or international, for that matter.

Local is perhaps best described as provincial. I recall an amusing incident in the beautiful English town of Bath. I was staying at a hotel called St Monica's. One morning, when I went down for breakfast, I asked the receptionist if I could borrow a copy of the newspapers. (When in Rome, do as the Romans do. So in Bath, which is characteristically Roman, do as the English do: read the newspapers during breakfast.) She smiled, very sweetly indeed, and said with a chuckle, "Oh, they've all been borrowed. I've only one left and I don't think you really want to read it." She took it out anyway and placed it on the counter. "It's a *local* paper," she said with a wink. "Full of scandals." Managing to keep a straight face, I said, "Thank you. I'll take it."

62
ACRONYMS & ABBREVIATIONS

Singaporeans love short forms, which are useful when everyone understands what everyone else is saying.

Drive around and you will see signs such as ECP (East Coast Parkway) and PIE (Pan Island Expressway). And someone wrote to the *Straits Times* and asked why Bukit Timah Expressway is BKE (and not BTE). Then there is CTE for Central Expressway and SLE for Seletar Expressway.

Airline geography abbreviates the names of airline destinations to three letters: SIN for Singapore, KUL for Kuala Lumpur, BKK for Bangkok, HKG for Hongkong, TYO for Tokyo, SYD for Sydney, BOM for Bombay, ZRH for Zurich, PAR for Paris, ROM for Rome, FRA for Frankfurt, LHR for London Heathrow, NYC for New York, SFO for San Francisco, LAX for Los Angeles and HNL for Honolulu. There seems to be a certain inexplicable logic in selecting the codes (the same kind in operation when Bukit Timah Expressway was named BKE and not BTE). But do you know that YVR stands for Vancouver and YTO for Toronto? Yet there seems to be apparent order in the system.

The airlines are themselves known by three-letter or two-letter codes, such as SIA or SQ for Singapore Airlines, QF for Qantas, CPA or CX for Cathay Pacific Airways, BA for British Airways and MAS or MH for Malaysian Airways System. But have you heard of 9P, short for Pelangi Air?

Where I work, there is a popular abbreviated term for idling or malingering, which is KLKK (*kia lai kia ki* in Hokkien, literally *walk here walk there*). Almost a secret code unknown to the bosses.

Our obsession with acronyms can best be illustrated in a letter which my boss received when he was invited to sit on a working committee set up by a government ministry. The first item on the agenda was *suggestions of an acronym for the committee*. The committee never met and that meant one less entry for the dictionary of Singapore acronyms.

That should bring some relief to a reader who wrote to the *Straits Times* (9 February 1995), protesting, "Why does Singapore practise the irritating habit of reducing phrases and names to initial letters?" He cited the examples of PCN for Telecom's Personal Communications Network, the Housing Board's REFS for Registration for Flat System and SAM for Singapore Art Museum. Interestingly, another letter in the same Forum Page, a reply from the Registry of Vehicles, was printed under the header: "Car owners not required to insure COE and Parf values". Chances are most people are more familiar with COE than Certificate of Entitlement, but it takes a while before the average person figures out that Parf is short for Preferential Additional Registration Fee.

63
NAMES & BUILDINGS

A building used to be nothing more than a building and, if it deserved a name, it was called XYZ Building: Yen San Building, Ocean Building, Cathay Building ...

And then it became fashionable to name these landmark buildings *Houses*, not just because most of them housed several tenants that filled the landlord's coffers but because *House* assumed a certain dignity (Parliament House, for example) and gave one a sense of belonging. Thus we have Shaw House, Shing Kwan House and Rubber House.

Then along came the importance of being central, and many buildings became *Centres*, such as Shaw Centre, People's Park Centre, Funan Centre and Clifford Centre. In later years, building names evolved into even more focussed points: Centrepoint, Northpoint, Chinatown Point ...

Over the years, size became the hallmark of any building set to make a name for itself. And buildings became huge complexes: People's Park Complex is one example. Huge grew into humongous, and cities loomed with notable names like Raffles City, Marina City and Ngee Ann City.

Our buildings have always competed to reach the sky, sprouting towers: Liat Towers, Shaw Towers, Shell Towers…

Vogue names include *court*, *plaza* and *square*. I am not sure if Colombo Court is so called because of its proximity to the High Court; think of Liang Court, which is but a stone's throw from the Subordinate Courts. *Court* does assume a certain air of sovereignty, yet it's as homely as *house* when you think of a European courtyard. Plaza, which is Spanish in origin but an American influence, is really an open square. In Singapore, some plazas are City Plaza, Plaza Singapura and International Plaza.

The in-name today is *Junction* as we return to basics and yearn for simplicity. If a building is located at the junction of two roads, why not call it so? There is Junction 8 in Bishan, and Bugis Junction is yet another eminent Singapore landmark.

64
MORE ON BUILDINGS

The first time that I came across the word *condotel* was in the heart of Bangkok when my Thai friend pointed out to me an apartment block under construction. "It is a new concept in building," he explained. "A combination of condominium and hotel." In other words, I suppose, service apartments with condominium facilities.

Soon after I returned to Singapore, I found a developer working on the same concept to market its project. Somehow, it didn't really catch on, probably because one was never quite clear of its real purpose. I understand it has now moved on across the Causeway to West Malaysia.

Condotel may not be a made-in-Singapore concept, but our planners have given us other equally interesting architectural concoctions, such as *distripark*. That, I take it, comes from a clever marriage between *distribution* and *park*. And if you visit one of these complexes at Pasir Panjang where many companies rent space for warehousing, you will quickly understand the genesis of the word.

Void deck, I am told, is uniquely Singaporean. This refers to the vacant space on the ground level of a block of HDB flats. And what used to be known simply as blocks are now given that little touch of elegance associated with *condo living* (*condo* is, of course, short for condominium and often so used) when dressed up as *apartments* or, a cross between the two living styles, *apartment blocks*. There was a time when some people used, rightly or wrongly, *blocks* and *flats*

THE VOID DECK!

TRIGG

to designate subsidised, public housing and *apartments* when they meant the more expensive and exclusive private developments. So you see, the name matters!

65
THE FOUR WORLDS

Once upon a time, there were four worlds of fun in Singapore. The first was Happy World, and this was followed by the Gay World, the Great World and the New World.

They were amusement parks, treats for the children. But I'm told that they were treats for grown men too, for they all featured one thing: cabarets where men took numbers to dance the *dondang sayang* or *joget* with numbered hostesses waiting in the queue.

Gay World was so named in the days when *gay* meant *happy*, to compete with its forerunner, Happy World. There was even a pop group of four men who happily called themselves the Gay Lads. Just as well they faded out of the limelight when the new Gay movement changed our understanding of being happily gay!

New World later became the site of the unfortunate Hotel New World which collapsed and took some lives. I was told by some people in Hong Kong (where there is also a Hotel New World) – those people who are the masters of superstition – that the *new* world could be interpreted as the *next* world, or the world a person enters after death. Among those who escaped the Singapore disaster were a couple who were rudely interrupted by the rumbling; both were married but not to each other.

Some readers might point out the existence of another world in Singapore, Beauty World. That is only a shopping centre, hardly the colourful arena of entertainment that the other worlds once offered.

66
SIGNS OF THE TIME

I cannot resist writing about some of the signs that I see in Singapore.

Sign #1 at Telok Ayer Street in the heart of Chinatown: *Famous Manipulator.* He is someone good with his hands, an expert in fixing (manipulating?) bones. A chiropractor.

Sign #2 at the crossroads of Rochor and North Bridge Roads: *Virgin Trading.* This sign shouldn't surprise anymore, since Richard Branson has launched Virgin Atlantic Airlines, named after the Virgin label in his music empire. But I understand the airline had a trying time translating the name into Chinese when its operations included Hong Kong. Any reference to that uncorrupt maiden state, if not tastefully done, can offend and spell trouble. In superstitious Hong Kong, the choice of a name can make or break a business.

Sign #3 along Changi Road: *Prawn Eating House.* Go on and have a good laugh – that seafood-loving house is still there. It reminds me of a friend who says he is a Hokkien speaking Cantonese. A hyphen would help clarify his meaning, but only visually and not when he speaks: so is he a Hokkien-speaking Cantonese, or a Hokkien (who is) speaking Cantonese?

Sign #4 at Telok Ayer Street: *Culture Association.* It is a shop that sells books, stationery and art materials as opposed, probably, to trashy magazines and works with no soul.

Sign #5 at Bencoolen Street: *Camera Hospital.* The proprietor will repair your *sick* camera. There will be ward charges, I suppose. I am told that this hospital has moved to new premises at Paradiz Centre, and I wonder if it took along with it the familiar green cross symbol.

Sign #6 along East Coast Road: *TST Medical Hall.* A grand term for a small shop that sells Chinese medicine – herbal, animal and otherwise. There are lots of these shops in HDB housing estates, and you need a strong stomach to take in the sights of some of the displays: deer antlers, rhinoceros horns, a tiger's penis soaked in a yellow solution, dried unidentifiable insects and snakes all curled up in bottles.

Sign #7 at East Coast Park: *Sorry, For Inconvenience This Way Please.* No apologies for any misinterpretation. What a difference a little comma makes!

Sign #8 at a food stall in Bedok: *Everyday Come Duck Rice*. It may sound all right and auspicious in Chinese *(Tian Tian Lai Ya Fan)*, but its English translation seems kind of odd. Just as strangely interesting too is how some hawkers advertise their fare: *organ soup* (curious foreigners may be revolted by this), *boneless duck* (ever seen ducks without bones waddling about, as if they are bred in the same way that seedless grapes and watermelons are cultivated?) and *economical rice and dishes* (who or what is being economical?)

67
ANG MO KIO

Its size baffles, its grid road system impresses and its name amuses. Some vernacular quarters think it was once a fertile ground for tomatoes (*ang mo kio* is Hokkien for *tomato*), but it is really named after a bridge (*ang mo kio* in Hokkien is also English Bridge). Why an English bridge, no one really knows. And what an unlikely place – before or after its development – to be finding an Englishman!

A more likely place is the Botanic Gardens, which was once known among the Chinese as the English Gardens, probably because of the way it was planned and because it was a popular strolling spot for leisurely English gentlemen and ladies. The local folks already had their *kampung* complete with shrubs, flowers, birds, butterflies, ducks, ponds, and, of course, an abundance of trees bearing fruits such as the *jambu ayer*, *chiku*, guava and soursop. The soursop is, in Hokkien, *ang mo lew lian* or the English durian. Any Englishman, I believe, will balk at the suggestion that it is like the durian that we know: the soursop is odourless compared to the pungent smell of the spiky fruit.

68
KING GEORGE V PARK

When I was a child, going to the King George V Park bounded by Tank Road and River Valley Road was a treat, although my siblings and I had been warned that the park was haunted. There were several stories of people who went there to commit suicide, hanging from the trees. We were, however, encouraged by the fact that there were more courting couples there than the occasional dead body.

Today the park has been renamed Central Park. It is hardly as notorious as the park by the same name in New York, but in my childhood, walking through the wooded garden in the dark was as exciting as riding a ghost train. Then, it was known to the Chinese residents in the vicinity by different names. One name was the regal *King's Foothill* (since it was difficult translating George V into Chinese) and another revealed its less flattering attribute as a place where *mosquitoes bite legs* (in Hokkien, *bang ka kah*). I don't recall being that badly bitten though.

69
THINGS AQUAMARINE

Call this a sick joke if you wish. It was a teaser a Singaporean posed us when my friends and I, ourselves true-blue Singaporeans, met him in Rome: "What do you call a virgin homosexual?"

We were stumped.

"Aquafresh!"

While he rolled over with infectious laughter, I was thinking of my favourite brand of toothpaste. I'm not sure if Smith Kline Beecham Corporation would relish the association. As far as I'm concerned, I always like its fresh aftertaste.

Unfortunately, *Ah Qua* is an unpleasant Singapore slang, used with contempt to refer to a homosexual man, usually one who is effeminate. Not anything marine, as its sound may suggest.

Singapore Lifestyle

70
GREETINGS

Food features prominently in Chinese culture. So one Chinese greets another, no matter what the time of day, with *Have you eaten?* It is imperative that the stomach be filled. Otherwise, that person is either pitiable (literally starving, being poor) or contemptible (if he has to go a-begging for alms, losing all self-respect).

The Malays greet one another with *Apa khabar?* or *What is the news?* Whatever the nature of the news, the other person is expected to reply, *Khabar baik* or *The news is good.* If there is bad news, it takes second place. Always, first the good news.

I suppose it is no different from the Englishman's *How do you do?* Invariably the greeted party will respond, *I'm fine, thank you.* Nobody really pauses to ponder if at all he is anything but fine. Don't tell me your troubles!

You might conclude that the English always talk about the weather, the Malays have unshaken faith in Allah and the Chinese are always making sure they don't go hungry.

71
RESPECT FOR AGE

Respect for age ranks high in the hierarchy of Asian values. It serves to remind a young person that without his forefathers, he would not have been born.

The Chinese react to disrespect for one's elders with the utmost disdain. The expression often used with reference to such gross misconduct is *Not big, not small* (*Bu da bu xiao*).

Not knowing the obvious difference between big and small is an inexcusable character flaw.

72
EXCUSE ME, MISS

If, in a restaurant, you hear someone beckoning a waitress, "Excuse me, Miss …" or simply "Miss …" you can almost be sure he is Singaporean.

Nothing really wrong with that. Some customers prefer to raise their hands and crack their knuckles. And still others clap their hands, as if summoning their serfs.

Silence, of course, speaks volumes. Don't forget to tap the table three times with a finger when someone pours you tea: it means *thank you*. I am told that this practice is not really Singaporean but Chinese, originating from a tale about an Emperor who journeyed through the land incognito and used only sign language to communicate with his men.

73
TOWKAYS

The man who owns the provision shop where you buy your rice and sugar is a towkay. The fishmonger at the market stall may address all his male customers as towkays. If someone is unsure of your status but suspects you to be a big shot, he is safe calling you a towkay – just as your boss is your towkay. So, it seems, anybody can be a towkay.

Strictly speaking, a towkay is a man of wealth, and with wealth comes power. And since it is said that behind every successful man is a woman, anyone who wants to be in the towkay's good books ought to heed the might and influence of the *towkay neo* (i.e., the towkay's wife).

74
HAINANESE RELATIONS

A pork seller addresses my mother as *suki*. You can tell at once that the stall holder is talking to a Hainanese Chinese. Calling a person *suki* is a neighbourly gesture. The word, literally translated, is *by the side of the house*, hence someone who lives next door.

The Hainanese community is known to be closely knit. Because they are a minority, the members in the community feel elated meeting one of their kind, hence the often-used term of *ka ki nan* (literally *our own people*). Some people think if a Hainanese person makes the order at a Hainanese restaurant, claiming the *ka ki nan* relation and speaking in Hainanese, he gets the best deal: quantity, quality and good service. And the rest in the party only stand to benefit.

75
BROTHERS & SISTERS

The communists feel banded together as comrades. But the wave of comradeship seems to have outlived its time. I was speaking to a Chinese teacher from Beijing and he confessed that the word *comrade* is no longer fashionable.

What surprised me was a letter issued by a trade union in Singapore to its members, addressing them not as comrades but as brothers and sisters. While we profess that the world should hold hands and embrace each other as belonging to one big family, I cannot help but feel a little queasy when the poultry seller at the market calls out to me, "Brother, today's chicken very good. Buy one, okay?" And to a female customer, he hollers, "Sister, this one I give you good price. Not so fat one, sister, good one."

To the poultry seller and others who use that affectionate brotherly and sisterly form of address, it is respect. No doubt about it. But I guess its appropriateness is determined by place. In church, somehow it sounds perfectly wholesome when the priest preaches, "Dear brothers and sisters …"

76
UNCLES & AUNTIES

Caucasians are apt to find this strange, if not baffling.

In Singapore, we usually address an older man who bears no blood relation at all to us as *uncle*, especially if he is a family friend. It is a respectable form of address. And for an older woman, it is *auntie*. And so it seems that on our island, almost everyone is related.

BIG SISTER
NOT AUNTIE!

TRIGG

The formal address of Mr or Mrs So-and-so is seldom invoked outside the office or official circles. I remember addressing a neighbour as Mrs Tan and being rebuked – in a friendly manner – for being so formal. She said, "We neighbour-neighbour don't have to be so formal lah; call me *Auntie* will do." And children visiting their friends at home will respect their friends' parents as *uncles* and *aunties*. Courting couples included. I suppose, claiming relations, however distant, and even if they are nonexistent, does bring people closer together.

77
COUSIN BROTHER

I'm always stumped by the reference to *cousin brother*, used predominantly by Chinese language speakers.

The Chinese language makes precise differentiation between a male and a female cousin, whether he or she is older or younger, and whether he or she is paternally or maternally related. Male cousins are either *biao ke* (older, maternal), *biao di* (younger, maternal), *tang ke* (older, paternal) or *tang di* (younger, paternal), and female cousins are either *biao che* (older, maternal), *biao mei* (younger, maternal), *tang che* (older, paternal) or *tang mei* (younger, paternal).

But *cousin brother* (as with *cousin sister*) is a Singaporean (and I suspect, Malaysian too) attempt to emphasise the specific relationship, literally translated but only partially. It adopts the word *cousin* as an adjectival qualifier equivalent to *biao* and *tang*. Hence, *cousin brother* tells only a small part of the story; it is either *biao ke* or *biao di* or *tang ke* or *tang di*.

78
AH HUAY & AH BENG

In the sixties, bell-bottoms (I'm referring to pants) were a rave among both men and women. And they came to an ignominious end as *road sweepers* and were considered *obiang* or *offbeat* (OB for short). Then, the *offbeat cha-cha* along with the *a-go-go* were popular tea dances at joints such as The Pink Pussycat and Gino's A-Go-Go.

Obiang refers predominantly to things unfashionably Chinese (*ching chong* or *chee-na*, the latter deliberately so pronounced). The *obiang* are sneered at by youths proud of the western influences in their heritage and background and by those injected with doses of self-assumed elitism rooted in a misplaced pride of being considered not so Chinese. Ah, therein sprouted the Pinkerton Syndrome! And *Ah Huay* and *Ah Beng* (Hokkien names: the female and male equivalents) – the way they dressed, styled their hair, spoke and behaved, the things they liked and even the activities they preferred and enjoyed – became the butt of jokes and contempt.

I object strongly to making fun of a person's name; it is the surest way of destroying his self-respect. And it is cruel. I was always careful about it when I was a teacher, and I take my hat off to the reporter who said she would not change her name and call herself Michelle, Melissa or Marjorie just because she was an *Ah Huay* (and she was). Good on you, Miss Teo Lian Huay!

Thank goodness, with the revival of interest in Chinese culture and things Chinese, and with the politicians extolling the virtues of Confucianism and decrying the decadent ways of the West, the ugly *obiang* has been finally laid to rest.

79
BHAI, CHOPE!

There was a time in the sixties when the sight of a turban could cause some excitement in the city, when little boys who had never heard of computer games amused themselves with things and people. The Sikh man became the subject of an easy-to-play game.

Chance was an important factor. Whoever first caught sight of a turbaned Sikh would quickly hit (or slap or tap) the head of the person next to him, chanting at the same time, *Bhai, chope!* That was his insurance against being similarly hit. If there were more than two persons present, the second person would quickly pass it down. And on and on, until it reached the last person, who obviously became the biggest loser of them all because he had no other head to slap.

The game honed one's alertness and the quickness of the hand. And Sikh men were not all that uncommon a sight in those days! They have outlived the game, though.

80
MAMA, AFFECTIONATELY

I used to wonder why some people call our Indian friends *mama*. I was cautious about using the term myself lest it was racist and derisive.

One day I asked an Indian colleague what *mama* stood for, and was quite surprised to learn that, far from being disrespectful, it means *uncle*.

I have not got around to calling an Indian friend *mama*, which I reserve with affection for mothers, whatever the race.

Yet there is no better description for the corner sundries shop (which may not be located in a corner) than the *mama* shop. It is operated by an Indian and sells the most surprising things sometimes, besides a variety of magazines, candy and *kanas*, glass marbles, light bulbs and condoms. If you survey closely enough the tight display of articles spread out on plywood tables, in glass cupboards and on open shelves, you may even find paper balls and true-to-life rubber snakes and spiders to scare the wits out of somebody you don't quite like.

Don't you sneer at the small-time operations of the *mama* shop though. At a time when most shops are closed and you really need something urgently, that is where you can often go for help. And children with only a few coins to spare will always find it such a treat to visit the *mama* shop.

81
RED-HAIRED DEVIL

When Alfonso d'Albuquerque and his Portuguese mates landed in Malacca in 1511, the natives called them white Bengalis. They were large, sharp-featured and wore beards like the dark-skinned traders who came from India, except that they were white.

The early British earned a different kind of reputation in Hong Kong, where people referred to them contemptuously as *hong mo gwai* or *gwai-lo*. Literally translated, *gwai* is *devil*, and a *hong mo gwai* is a red-haired devil. It refers to all whites, as orientals very quickly discovered that the British were not the only fair-skinned people. The name stays to this day, and is commonly used where the Cantonese proliferate, and that includes Singapore. The Hokkien equivalent *ang mo quee* is also popular. Since many Caucasians became good friends, the reference to *quee* or devil was discreetly dropped; they became simply *ang mo*.

Some Caucasians take offence to the *gwai lo* nomenclature, no different from *Chink* for a Chinese, *nigger* for a black, *pommy* for an Englishman and *Jap* for a Japanese or *Honkies* for the inhabitants of Hong Kong, who prefer to be known as Hongkongers, if not British subjects. But the Americans somehow do not seem to feel as offended by the *Yankee* label.

82
PERANAKAN PATOIS

The Peranakan patois is an interesting blend of different tongues, when the Straits-born Chinese *campur* English, Malay and predominantly Hokkien words in an apparently incongruous but tasty *rojak*.

You can learn much about it, watching a Peranakan soap, which is usually a tear-jerker. Two women and a man carry the plot: a strong mother, a feeble son and his jealous wife. The central figure is the matriarch, who rules the family but *sayang* and *manja* the son. And then the son *kahwin* and invariably becomes torn between his mother and his wife. He does not want to be seen to *pakat* with either one of the women. *Aiyoh*, it is so sad when such a terrible thing like that happens!

"Chilaka!" shrieks the matriarch and complains bitterly about her *pai mia* because of a disrespectful daughter-in-law (she never blames her good-for-nothing son) who doesn't even know how to cook *hee piao soup*, *babi ponteng* and *ayam buah keluak*; and the daughter-in-law cannot see how hers is a *ho mia* with an unreasonable mother-in-law (and blames her husband for hanging on to the string of his mother's apron). Poor man, indeed! Really *bo piang si!*

The matriarch, of course, has many advisors: *Ah Chim*, *Tua Ee* and *Bibiks* of many names. They are really the *kay pohs* who will not hesitate to *cucuk*. The language becomes incisive and vitriolic as the drama climaxes, and bucketfuls of tears are spilled on and off stage. The audience loves it. And when enough tears have poured, the wife repents, the matriarch forgives and the son slips into obscurity. The *ho sim* advisors sing a different tune and join in the celebration. And there is good news: the wife is pregnant. Everybody loves a happy ending. And the *nonyas* and *babas* go home, feeling completely satisfied.

I have always wondered why the matriarch of a Peranakan soap is often played by a man in drag, except so far, as far as I know, for the soliloquist *Emily of Emerald Hill*. I think that the Peranakan *wayang* is no different from the Chinese street opera or Shakespearean plays of history, when women were seldom seen or accepted on stage and young boys had to take on the female roles. But, of course, the Peranakan matriarch demands a stronger character player than a boy or even a young man, and G.T. Lye and Kenny Chee are hot favourites from the pins in their hair to the sequined slippers they wear.

In case anyone points an accusing finger at me and says that I *bedek*, I beg your pardon. I am no Peranakan myself.

***

Peranakan Glossary

campur: mix

rojak: a mixed salad, hence an unlikely concoction of different things

sayang: dotes on

manja: spoils; pampers

kahwin: marry

pakat: collude

aiyoh: meaningless expression like *oh!*

chilaka: a really bad swear word

pai mia: bad life

hee piao soup, babi ponteng, ayam buah keluak: Peranakan dishes *ho mia:* good life

bo piang si: can't be helped

Ah Chim, Tua Ee, Bibiks: women relatives and friends

kay pohs: busybodies; people who meddle in other people's affairs

cucuk: Malay colloquial term for stab in the back, hence cause trouble

ho sim: good-hearted or kind

nonyas: Peranakan women

babas: Peranakan men

wayang: stage show or opera; sometimes used figuratively as a verb to mean put up a show (pretend)

bedek: lie; bluff

83
GOO-GOO GAA-GAA

Parents and other adults tend to *goo-goo gaa-gaa* when they talk to babies.

Here is a common infant talk list:

"Daddy will bring you out to *walk-walk*."

"Come and *play-play* with John-John."

"You make Mommy *wet-wet* (when the child urinates)."

"*Eat-eat* your rice, Darling."

"The porridge is *hot-hot* (or *nice-nice* or *good-good*)."

"You are *naughty-naughty* because you *spill-spill* the orange juice on the carpet."

"If you don't behave yourself, Mommy will *beat-beat* you."

Talk about double-vision; what about hearing double?

84
SPEAK MANDARIN CAMPAIGN

Taxi-drivers have their own brand of humour. A cynical operator had this to say about the Speak Mandarin Campaign: "*Jiang huayi? Aiya, better jiang chuaji.*" (*Jiang huayi* is Mandarin for *Speak Mandarin* whereas *jiang chuaji* is adulterated to mean *talk money*: *chuaji* in Hokkien is *dollars*).

85
QIPAO OR CHEONGSAM?

Sari for the Indians, *baju kurung* and *sarung kebaya* for the Malays and *qipao* for the Chinese.

Qipao?

It will take another generation as we switch to *hanyu pinyin* before we are comfortable about substituting *qipao* for *cheongsam* (a Cantonese word), the traditional, high-collared long gown with high slits on the sides. Someone once said that a woman dressed in a *cheongsam* is more seductive than a woman who wears little or nothing to cover her skin, because the *cheongsam* teases and tempts. Working on the imagination is a very powerful seductive ploy.

Lest you forget, there is also the common but less fashionable *samfoo* which is fast losing its popularity among Chinese women.

86
THE POLITE CIVIL SERVANT

Many years ago, I received this note from the Estates & Lands Division of the HDB: "Dear Sir/Madam, I beg to acknowledge receipt of your letter dated 22/9/77 and to state that the contents are noted."

A friend who was working as an EO (Executive Officer) with the Board told me they had engaged a letter-writing expert to conduct English classes for senior staff dealing with the public.

The note referred to is, of course, by now archaic, but the style of writing survives in official notes, not necessarily confined to the HDB, that many of us still receive.

87
POLICE STORY

In London, he is the bobby. In Singapore, he is the *mata-mata*; appropriately so, because *mata* in Malay means eye, and policemen are the eyes of the law.

Unfortunately, the policeman in Singapore is a much feared man. His job appears to be one of arresting rather than helping people in maintaining law and order. When disciplining their naughty children, parents are apt to warn them that "police (or *mata-mata*) will catch you". So children grew up being wary of the men in midnight blue who wield batons, revolvers and handcuffs.

For some years now the Singapore Police Force has tried to improve the image of the policeman as the friendly neighbourhood man. Riding a bicycle somehow seems to have softened that image of a man who used to ride in a black *maria* screaming through the streets. Maybe if more of them are seen helping old folks and young children cross the busy streets, their image might improve.

88
SAMSENG: AH SENG OR SAM?

A *samseng* is a gangster, thug, hooligan or hoodlum.

He is most likely a Chinese, whose name may be Ah Seng. If he is known to be *yankee* (fashionably attired, presumably like an American, with a penchant for tight jeans and star-studded cowboy boots), he may choose to call himself Sam. (No reference to the famed Singapore Cowboy who has a penchant for singing country and western songs.)

No mother will want her son to behave like a *samseng* or her daughter to befriend one, because that spells trouble. In the sixties, he was usually a member of some secret society when flash gang fights and triad clashes were frequent.

89
DISTANT COUSINS & RHYMES

(1) The Karang Guni Man

Have you seen the *karang guni man* of late? These days he comes round not on foot but by bike or driving a lorry. With the amount of garbage that our households discard daily, it would appear a thriving business. His English cousin is, of course, the rag-and-bone man.

(2) The Satay Man

What about the *satay man* who lives in Sandy Lane? If you haven't heard of him, ask your children. They may still sing about him in school: "Do you know the satay man who lives in Sandy Lane?"

He has an English cousin too, though they trade in different food. Our *satay man* sells meat on bamboo skewers, the meat dipped in a chilli-hot peanut sauce as you eat it, but his English cousin has his fingers in flour. He is the muffin man from Drury Lane.

(3) There Was A Man In Tanjong Katong

When I was invited to give a lunch talk on a topic of my choice, I spoke on the beauty and power of language, quoting *The Psalms of David* and lines from Shakespeare's *Macbeth*, the works of Wordsworth and Kahlil Gibran's *The Prophet*.

To encourage participation, I introduced my audience to some saucy limericks and invited them to play with rhymes. This was the result, the less saucy type:

There was a man in Tanjong Katong
Who loved to eat lontong.
He married a wife from Hong Kong
And had a son they called King Kong.
Together they played ping pong
All day long …

There were many suggestions and I had to check their enthusiasm. I have no doubt that the man in Tanjong Katong had many distant limerick relatives too.

90
DOLLY PARTON & CHICKEN BREASTS

Singaporeans do have a good sense of humour, albeit sometimes leaning on the saucy side.

The TGIF restaurant at Far East Plaza has a colourful menu that uses vivid imagery to describe its servings, one of which is the Dolly Parton special: chicken breasts. No explanation needed. Many men find the *Nine-to-Five* actress

simply gorgeous, and a colleague of mine goes "oooh" whenever he sees an image of her, saying he can't help but recall *Islands in the Stream*, the popular song she sang with Kenny Rogers.

Chicken is a popular food among Singaporeans, served any style. And a favourite word among them too. The *Oxford Advanced Learner's Dictionary* lists it as slang for *coward*. Our party at the TGIF were tickled by the menu, and the colleague who dug both the bird and the country singer *chickened out* on the Dolly Parton special.

"Shy lah!" our colleague confessed and asked for a spring chicken instead.

91
JUMBO FOR SIZE

There was a time when it was fashionable to go for things *jumbo*. The Boeing makers were making a name for their jumbo jets, and it looked like the ultimate in size.

So the jumble sale became a *jumbo* sale. A *hokkien mee* soup vendor boasted *jumbo* prawns to go with the noodles. There were *jumbo* TV screens, *jumbo* posters and *jumbo* diamonds. Indeed, *jumbo* anything to impress.

Businessmen were quick to name their enterprises Jumbo. The Singapore Phone Book lists a dozen businesses so christened: Jumbo Crafts, Jumbo Decorations & Supplies, Jumbo Department Store, Jumbo Diamond House, Jumbo Investigation & Security, Jumbo Jewellery Manufacturers, Jumbo Navigation, Jumbo Coffee House, Jumbo Realty, Jumbo Seafood, Jumbo Shipping and Jumbo Transportation. A motley group, but none of them related to Disney's Dumbo the elephant.

If Boeing could be considered the trendsetter in this respect, it is *mega* in the eighties. It started as an apt description for the likes of Michael Jackson and Tom Cruise, those *mega* stars that make *mega* bucks. And it has become a useful word in today's business. A supermarket in Jurong upgraded itself as a *megamart*. Wrote futurists Alvin and Heidi Toffler in a *New York Times* article which was re-printed in Singapore's *Business Times* (29 August 1994): "Mergers are declared and cancelled and new alliances announced almost every day ... How much sense do these *mega-marriages* make?"

92
THE BALD PATE

First there was Yul Bryner with his imposing portrayal of a Siamese emperor in *The King And I*. Then along came Telly

Savalas as detective Kojak. And, of course, *kungfu* disciple David Carradine. Even Joan Chen sported that clean look.

An Indian colleague with a fast balding pate once disclosed a nickname his Chinese pals had given him. It meant *emperor,* he announced proudly. Some friends indeed! I had to tell him that *guang tou* is literally *bald head.* He didn't mind; Chinese emperors were usually shaved bald when they were young. To him, the bald pate is synonymous with being an emperor.

Not so, however, in Singapore with *botak* or *botak head.*

93
MINDING OTHER PEOPLE'S BUSINESS

The Chinese *kay poh* is the English busybody, one who always minds other people's business. With due respect to its residents, I do wonder how a road in popular District 9 is named Kay Poh Road.

Don't, however, confuse *kay poh* with *chai poh.*

An ugly scene stays vivid in my mind, a cruel incident on an old Hock Lee bus. A dark, skinny woman, quite old by the wrinkles on her face but all dolled up, was slow in getting off the bus, moving like a prima donna conscious of her appearance and touching her scanty permed hair now and then to make sure no strand was loose. As soon as she alighted, the impatient conductor grunted in Hokkien, "Old like *chai poh* and yet so *hiao.*"

Chai poh is a dried, salted vegetable that looks brown and shrivelled. *Hiao* can best be described as vain and flirtatious. Such a woman is said to be inviting trouble from men.

94
A STARING INCIDENT

A visiting Caucasian friend was puzzled by a report that a man had been stabbed to death in a staring incident.

"What led to the stabbing?" she asked.

I explained: "He stared at another man who retaliated by plunging a knife into his body."

It wasn't really an eye for an eye, but a stab for a stare. One ought to be careful about how one uses one's eyes.

95
FACE

A matter of face is something to be handled delicately.

Face is very important in the East, typically Asian and very much so Chinese. It is more than just what a person looks like; it is how he looks.

If a man has no pride in his face, then he has no right to be himself. He might as well walk around with a sack over his head. That probably best explains the meaning of the expression *nowhere to hide one's face* when a person is embarrassed or feeling shame. In such a delicate situation, it is said that he has *lost face*. And the consequences can be disastrous.

In any dealings, business or pleasure, the Chinese attach much value to *face*. One mustn't cause another person to *lose face*, and attempts to *save face* have led to feuds resulting in deaths. No amount of face-lift can disguise that burning colour of a face lost (although it might well be pale) or make good the damage inflicted.

A man's face is his dignity, if not fortune.

96
A LADIES' MAN

By definition, obviously he is a man much liked by the women. But his fellow men (need I emphasise, *male* fellow men) view his charm differently, with envy and contempt. In my university days, he was branded a *smeller*. An unpleasant term, no different from a *sniffler*. And all just because he has a good nose and the scent of a woman never escapes it.

97
WIFE OR LOVER?

Ai ren is not Singaporean, but the term stumps or even embarrasses many a Singaporean when he converses with a Chinese from Beijing.

I was myself amused by a man's reference to his wife as *ai ren* when I met him in Beijing. That, to Singaporeans who speak some Chinese, is *lover* and, if you are already married, it suggests an illicit affair.

Indeed, why isn't a man's wife also his lover when she is someone he loves?

98
MAHJONG PLAYERS

Want to arrange a game of *mahjong?* Find out first if you have the *kakis*. Or, if you're invited and you're particular about the company, check out the *kakis*.

Kaki (Malay) is literally *leg*, and means player.

A mahjong table has four legs and a set of *mahjong* cards or tiles has four of everything including the winds from the four corners of the earth: north, south, east and west (the Chinese order is east, south, west and north). You build four walls with the cards before you begin to play. Four is therefore the ideal number of *kakis*, but there are some people who make do with only three.

99
BREAK A LEG

My wife's sister is an ardent fan of the theatre and is herself an accomplished stage actress. On the opening night of one of her performances, my mother-in-law called up her regular florist for a basket of flowers to be sent to the theatre with the message, "Break a leg."

The florist called her back after five minutes, obviously puzzled. "Did you say …?"

My mother-in-law confirmed that it was *break a leg*.

The florist must have thought that queer and cruel. Why would my mother-in-law wish her daughter to break a leg when she was going to perform on stage? She sent the flowers anyway, and was pleased to learn that the actress did not physically break a leg.

"No, she wasn't dancing," said my mother-in-law when asked by the florist after the event.

100
YAMSENG!

You cannot avoid this toast at any Chinese wedding dinner, and the louder the toasting, which usually comes in a train of three, the more celebrated the function. Sometimes it goes with the *yam* stretching ad infinitum, with one toasting master after another adding it on before the toasting collects in a crescendo of *seng*.

It doesn't sound quite like what it looks, but you can imagine its infectious repetition and the rowdiness: *"yam, yam, yam, yam, yam, yam, yam, yam, yam, yam... SENG!"*

I am told that *yam seng* is more Singaporean than Chinese, who have their comparatively more sober *kan bei* which has also been adopted by the Japanese. The English are gentler with their mild *bottoms up*.

The *yam seng* victim at a wedding dinner is usually the bridegroom when he has a teetotaller for a best man, and I hear the unfortunate story of a *new man* (that's what the Chinese call a bridegroom; the corollary is *new woman* for a bride) who was completely flushed out on his wedding night and had to lie in bed for five consecutive days! Never again, he vowed.

101
SOMETHING TO TAKE HOME

Don't be surprised if at the end of a dinner in a restaurant, the waitress walks up to you and asks, "Do you want to *ta pau*?" Waste not. It is perfectly normal and legitimate to *ta pau* unfinished food to bring home and eat another day. After all, you have already paid for it.

Most restaurants do a good *ta pau* job, placing the food in a decent takeaway box, nicely packaged with a string for your finger to slip through its loop. Cynics used to call it a doggy bag, but it is certainly not food meant only for the family dog.

But if you want to avoid having to *ta pau* food home, be judicious when you place the order. Do not think your stomach has the capacity of a camel and bite off more than you can chew.

102
HEATY OR COOLING OR WINDY?

When a Chinese physician diagnoses a patient's common ailment as caused by something *heaty* or *cooling*, most Chinese will tell you it is not balderdash but an analysis rooted in the *yin yang* principle. If a person's makeup is *heaty*, he needs a dose of *cooling* medicine to bring about the *yin yang* balance, and vice versa.

The Chinese classify foods we eat as having properties that are either *heaty* or *cooling*. Peanuts and ginger are *heaty*, so is curry. Barley, bittergourd, cucumber and watermelon are *cooling*. Strangely, beancurd is *cooling* but soybean milk is *heaty*. Durian is *heaty*, and it is said that eating the fruit while drinking liquor (e.g. brandy), which is also *heaty*, can be fatal. But mangosteens (dubbed the queen of fruits just as durian is known as the king of fruits), which are *cooling*, counteract the *heatiness* of durians. It is always wise to balance our intake of *heaty* and *cooling* foods; too much of one and too little of the other is not judicious.

When a person suffers from a cough that has been diagnosed as a *heaty* cough, he will be advised to drink lots of barley or *cheng t'ng* (a clear, sweet broth of herbal ingredients, lotus nuts and jelly) and lay off curry. But if it is a cough caused by the body being too *cool,* then he will need a concoction of different herbs to keep him warm. *Yang sheng*, a herbal root, is said to help combat heatiness, but *ginseng* can raise the heat. Women often complain about the *heatiness* of chocolates: "Look, pimples! And all I took was one small bar!"

It all seems so logical. And related to the weather.

Some people describe the material of a dress or some cloth as *cooling*, but that has nothing to do with Chinese medical science.

Some foods may be categorised as *windy* too. Such foods may cause too much air or wind to be trapped in the stomach, thereby causing undue stress and discomfort. They are not recommended for children and pregnant women, in particular. These foods include brinjals and a certain variety of banana although doctors and nutritionists schooled in western medical and food science will insist that a banana is a banana, whatever the species. Many of our grandmothers would disagree.

103
SALES

Singaporeans love sales, so do tourists who flock to the stores for cheaper than normal prices.

The attraction used to be just one big word (usually in bold red) – SALE – but competition has led to hoots of The Big Sale, The Sale of the Year, The Biggest Sale Ever, The Biggest Sale in Town, The Mega Sale, The Sale of Sales, The Sale That You Have Been Waiting For, The Sale of the Century and The Mother of all Sales (after Saddam Hussein's The Mother of all Battles; an issue of *A & M* (Asian Advertising and Marketing) headlines a story "The Mother of Ice Cream Wars Heats Up").

Some stores have sales all year round. If only shoppers knew when to rest their feet during the intervals that the shops take down one set of banners and put up another. There are, of course, many occasions for a sale: Opening Sale, Renovation Sale, Stock Clearance Sale, Closing Down

Sale, Removal Sale, New Year Sale (the beginning of a new calendar year), Chinese New Year Sale, Hari Raya Sale, Deepavali Sale, Christmas Sale, School Holiday Sale, National Day Celebration Sale, New Arrivals Sale, Anniversary Sale, Buy American or Australian Promotion (at discounted prices), Special Sale (unnamed) and even Summer Sale (yes, here in Singapore).

Discounts also attract shoppers, never mind if an unscrupulous store marks up its prices to mark them down. I made such a discovery when a big store advertised discounts of up to 70%: an item which I bought on a normal day would have cost more working in the discount! I have avoided that store since then and concentrate only on those honest ones which fortunately number in the majority.

Other sales gimmicks that attract include *Buy one, get one free*, *Free additional 250 gms*, free gifts (but only while stock lasts!), lucky draws (especially those with big prizes like a holiday for two in Europe or a 2000 cc car and those that guarantee *instant* wins), free samples and discount coupons.

In Singapore, there is never a dull day for shoppers.

104
PASAR MALAM

The *pasar malam* or night market invokes nostalgia for those who remember the street stalls of the sixties. As the name suggests, the market operated by night.

It was quite a treat moving from stall to stall, picking up bargains. A wide range of goods was available, usually small household products, clothes and accessories, watches and clocks, toys and food. With the clampdown on illegal hawking and a shift in shopping habits as more and more modern shopping centres started sprouting all over the island, these *pasar malam* stalls began to disappear.

Today they are back, more as a novelty, sometimes touted as tourist attractions in "Surprising Singapore", but in a controlled and organised manner at designated locations. The stalls may be grouped together in a square or on some open land (in which event they may be collectively advertised as a trade fair) and may not therefore line the roads as they used to in the early days. A wider range of goods is available but they are not necessarily cheaper. The stalls may also operate during or throughout the day, but to many people they are still the *pasar malam*.

It doesn't really matter what time of day it is, does it?

105
PLACES NEAR & FAR

I live next door to a childcare centre, so I learn as much as the children left in the care of a team of some three or four women whose voices are my morning alarm clock.

One day, the children were raising a din. One of the women screamed: "You're making so much noise like the market people!" No doubt about it, the bustling local market is a noisy place!

Another morning (and this happened when Saddam Hussein was waging a war on Kuwait), one of the women in charge threatened a wailing child: "If you don't stop crying, I'll send you to Iraq!" When I was a child, the threat was Timbuctoo. Others preferred Siberia. In the UK, it was probably Coventry, where the subject would be abandoned to social solitary. For the Chinese in Beijing, it would be Tianya Haijiao in Hainan Island. But for the folks on Christmas Island, it was Singapore.

A cousin who used to live on that beautifully named island in the Indian Ocean was taught a poem in the sixties about a child who would habitually not shut the door, thus letting in a cold draft; his parents threatened to deport him to Singapore. The writer, I presume, was thinking of a place far from Australia, and the child's name happened to be Godfrey Gordon Gustavus Gore, which rhymes with Singapore.

In Singapore, however, no one likes to be called a candidate for *Woodbridge*, a mental institution.

106
WET MARKET

You get it fresh at the wet market but frozen at the supermarket. That's probably how a number of Singaporeans shop for fish and fowl.

Not surprisingly, the wet market is usually wet. The floor, that is. Vendors are quite careless about the water they use at their stalls, perhaps to create the impression of freshness, that the fish is hardly out of its natural habitat and the fowl has only recently been slaughtered and washed. In the past, the fowl came all covered with feathers at the stalls, still clucking or quacking and pecking. There is fresh meat too (although cows and pigs never made it to the stalls in one piece), and vegetables that seem to have only just arrived from the farms. And of course, not forgetting freshly laid eggs!

The choice is yours: the wet market or the supermarket? Inevitably, one talks about fresh or frozen.

107
GUARANTEED QUALITY

Like most things, durians come in different grades. Prices range widely from as low as a dollar to as high as twenty-five dollars or thereabouts a fruit. Whether they are the *sampah* crops or fruits of the obscure but formidably named Tiger Hill, the best at any stall is the *bao jia* (Hokkien) or *bao chi* (Mandarin) variety. *Bao jia* or *bao chi* is the stamp of guaranteed quality. Literally translated, it is expressed awkwardly as *sure can be eaten*. Implied is the excellent quality of the fruit: not only 100% edible but good to eat.

Like fruit, like vendor. They are both quite naturally rough. The spiky durian shell is ugly and defies touch by the unguarded human hand. The durian vendor is usually aggressive and apt to display a nasty, explosive temper. He works quickly and deftly with a knife or slicer. He cracks a thin line down one side of the fruit and holds it under your nose, extolling its intoxicating fragrance. He may allow you to touch the pulp within, but only slightly, before he whisks it away and drops it into the sale bag. While it happens, you cannot squeeze in a word in agreement or protest, and by your silence he assumes your consent to buy. He then moves quickly to work on the second fruit. Remember his deftness with the knife, and try saying "no" at that juncture!

Durian customers, beware! Whether the fruit costs a dollar or twenty-five, and whether it comes with the *bao jia* or *bao chi* guarantee, the law of *caveat emptor* applies.

108
PROPERTY ADVERTISEMENTS

Housing agents employ their favourite stock phrases to create interest and, hopefully, boost sales. I picked these two advertisements from the Classifieds section of the *Straits Times*:

Advertisement #1

D.15 ALMOST SOLD! Exclusive lowrise apt. Choice unit. 1350 sq. ft. Split level. 3 + 1 rms. Fhold. $715,000 neg.

The ALMOST SOLD tag is supposed to act as an inducer, that the property is so good it is almost sold yet for some unknown reason it remains on the market. It can also arouse suspicion, that something is not quite right about it. No wonder many "almost sold" properties have passed from agent to agent and remain unsold over several weeks.

Advertisement #2

PRICED TO SELL! D.19 Chuan Park. 1851 sq. ft. 3 + 1 rms. High flr. Face North. Unblocked. Breezy. Good renovation. Well kept. F/aircon.

What properties, may I ask, are *not* priced to sell? With huge sums of money involved in property deals, it is difficult to fault buyers for being the three C's – cautious, choosy and critical.

109
HAVE THE CAKE & EAT IT

Singaporeans will prove to the sceptics that you can have your cake and eat it.

The story goes that a strange animal was discovered by a party comprising an American, a Britisher, a Frenchman, a Japanese and a Chinese. The Frenchman was concerned about naming the animal, the Britisher about studying its habitat and the American about protecting it from extinction. The Japanese whipped out his camera to photograph it and the Chinese was thinking up ways of cooking it.

Then along came a Singaporean.

He had no objection to the Frenchman naming the animal although he would have preferred the name in *hanyu pinyin*. He was prepared to learn from the Britisher but the myth of the Loch Ness monster loomed large in his mind. He supported the American endeavour to protect the animal from extinction although he couldn't understand the President's penchant for shooting wild ducks. Like the Japanese, he would have liked a photograph of the animal so long as he was in the photograph too. While accepting the Chinese man's invitation to an exotic feast, he would make sure that when the party was over, he would return home with some souvenir. A tooth maybe, or, better still, a wishbone.

Cross-Cultural Influences

110
A COMMON HERITAGE

In a multilingual society like ours, it is only to be expected that the various languages (including dialects) will cross-fertilise. Many words have become common property.

Take, for example, the humble bread, which is *roti* to Malays, Chinese, Indians and Eurasians alike. And in honour of our Caucasian friends, the local version of the hamburger – which looks nothing like the American version – has been named *Roti John*. There is also the *roti prata*, an Indian version of the pancake but eaten with curry instead of butter and jam or honey.

The Malays have adopted the Chinese *gua* to denote the first person. Money is *duit* (Malay) or *lui* (Hokkien), which are really the same word but pronounced slightly differently. Similarly, *loteng* (Malay) or *lau teng* (Hokkien) refers to a floor above (upstairs). The Hainanese and the Malays use *tuala* for towel, but the former have a word which has stumped many a Hokkien friend: *a-boo*, which is Hainanese for *apple* but Hokkien for *mother*. I suspect the Hainanese word is derived from the English *apple* itself. No harm done, since the *apple of one's eye* is always someone dearly loved.

On the other hand, *teh* and *kopi* are almost universally understood by all as tea and coffee. Patrons of the *sarabat stall* (once a common sight, a tea-and-coffee stall looking like a table on wheels with a roof, set up, usually by an Indian vendor, by the roadside) or the *kopi tiam* (Chinese for coffee shop) may be familiar with the terms *teh-o* or *kopi-o*: black or plain tea or coffee without milk. Sugar may be added. But if it is *teh-kosong* or *kopi-kosong*, even the sugar

is forgone, *kosong* being Malay for zero, nothing or empty. However, when the tea or coffee is served white, i.e., with milk added, it becomes *teh* or *kopi susu*; the waiter at the *kopi tiam* may prefer to scream the order as *teh* or *kopi guni*. *Susu* is Malay and *guni* is Hokkien for milk.

Somehow European and American visitors to my office always find it strange that when their orders for tea and coffee are taken they are often asked, "Black or white?" or "With milk and sugar?" They assume that beverages would be served with the complements of milk and sugar, which they would add themselves or have the option to ignore. And there are the first-timers who wonder why sugar and milk are absent when Chinese tea is being served.

Talking about tea and the *sarabat stall*, mention must be made of *teh tarek*. It is always a treat to see it prepared, the yellow tea stretching from cannister to cup, back and forth. (*Tarek* is Malay for *pull*.) The purpose of the antic is not so much to entertain as to cool the steaming hot tea.

111
COLOURS

In Chinese, it is perfectly acceptable to say *red colour* or *blue colour* or *green colour*, and by virtue of their Chinese background, many Singaporeans say: "I prefer *pink colour*." "The dress is *black colour*." "I want to buy a *blue colour* pen." The Englishman thinks that the colour speaks for itself. Hence, "I prefer pink." "The dress is black." "I want to buy a blue pen."

112
MAKAN TIME

Makan is Malay for eat, so "Let's go *makan*" means "Let's go eat."

The word is used freely, no matter what time of day it is, so long as a person is hungry or greedy. If it is midday, the *makan* connotes lunch, and if it is evening, the *makan* is dinner. Anytime a person wants to eat is *makan time*.

The meal voucher distributed to workers in some companies is commonly referred to as the *makan chit*.

One cannot deny that the average Singaporean loves to eat. When you talk to them about food, they may well ask you, "Does your mouth water?"

113
SOUP & MEDICINE

The Chinese have two very versatile words for the act of consuming food: *chi* (eat) for solids and *he* (drink) for liquids.

We eat rice. We eat dinner. And we drink wine. What about medicine, whether a solution or tablets? And what about soup, creamy or clear with vegetables and meat?

Singaporeans are apt to say "eat your medicine" but "drink up your soup". Never mind if the medicine is a dose of some red liquid or the soup is creamy with chunks of potatoes, carrots and meat.

114
MILK + WATER

One of the challenges I faced when I was teaching in a school in a poor neighbourhood – sadly a school the public was apt to dismiss as below average – was to help pupils think in English before speaking or writing. Almost all of them came from homes where only Chinese or Chinese with a smattering of English was spoken. But could I blame them for language mistakes when a Physics teacher in the school often said, "How *many* water can you pour into this beaker?"

That seemed a more serious flaw than when the students said *milk water*, which amused me somewhat. I believe that it is not incorrect to refer to that white liquid as *milk water* in Chinese, particularly when you think of a concoction made up of milk powder or condensed milk and water. It is therefore really milk + water, unless you mean fresh milk straight from the breast or udder.

What about *rainwater*? In a country where we have as much rainfall as sunshine, it is a term we commonly use. Somehow, we feel more comfortable saying "collect some *rainwater*" than "collect some rain". But, fear not, it is not a bad expression. *Rainwater*, as defined by the *Oxford Advanced Learner's Dictionary*, is "soft water that has fallen as rain, e.g. not taken from wells, etc." And in the days of yore, mothers in kampungs often warned their mischievous children not to play in *drainwater*, especially after a torrential downpour.

115
EYES SEE

The Chinese word for *see* is *kan*. Whether it is a person, a book or the TV, the Chinese use *kan*, but in English we *see* a person, *read* a book and *watch* (a show on) TV.

Nobody says "*see* a book" when he means "*read* a book", but many people are apt to say "*see* (instead of *watch*) TV".

116
PLEAS FOR HELP

Tolong is a very useful Malay word that has crept into the Chinese vocabulary. It is a plea for help.

Poor people often turn to the gods with pleas of *tolong*, that through their (gods') immortal intervention they (people) may strike it rich on the race course or at *toto*. So do not turn a deaf ear to pleas of *tolong*, be it from a pauper who begs for money to buy a meal or from a co-worker who needs help to complete an urgent assignment. The gods have eyes too.

117
IT'S YOUR FASAL

I have always thought that the word was *pasar* until a scholar
told me it should be *fasal*. So if it is your *fasal*, it is not my
problem. As a colleague who is not prepared to lend a helping
hand would say, "If you don't know how to do it, it's your
fasal." Or, when someone who prefers to stay on the sideline
tells you, "Go or don't go is your *fasal*, not mine."

In the case of the unsatisfied wife who wants to keep up
with the Lees and the Wongs next door and insists that her
husband buys her a diamond as bright and as big as Mrs
Lee's, it is her husband's *fasal* and not ours.

Big headache, some people may say. But some others
prefer the morbid "It's your *funeral*!"

118
WORDS THAT SPELL TROUBLE

There are no good substitutes for the Malay *susah* or *teruk*
and the Hokkien *jia lat*. When you are caught in such a
situation, you are in trouble. And it is not uncommon to
qualify these words with *very* for emphasis, hence "very
susah lah!"

An ex-colleague of mine who used to work in the kitchen
would scream instead "Pork chop!" No explanation is needed:
visualise what it is like to suffer a karate chop!

There is also the Hokkien-Malay intermarriage of *buay
tahan* (*BTH*, in short), which is literally "cannot tolerate or
stand it". It is amusing though, the context in which it is
commonly used:

Scenario One

The boss pressurises his staff and they throw in the towel. *"BTH,"* says one of them.

Scenario Two

A beautiful woman walks by a gathering of men, who immediately raise their brows and open their mouths with oohs and wahs. One of them adds, *"Buay tahan!"*

See the difference?

119
DEATH KNELL

To die is to reach the end, a point of no return.

So it is not difficult to understand why someone driven to the wall says, *"Die!"* The word hangs on many a trembling lip, expecting the worst: a student who is summoned to the principal's office, knowing he has done wrong; a worker who has not completed his assignment and faces a possible pay-cut or dismissal; a trickster who leaves clues in his trail; an engineer who releases a machine only to discover later that a crucial part is missing; a hen-pecked man who comes home reeking with alcohol, suspecting his wife to be waiting at the door!

In a similar situation, when someone drives you up the wall or gives you a tall order, you may throw your arms up in exasperation and scream *"Can die!"*

Die is a serious word and no laughing matter. Nothing can be worse than when someone is caught in this dilemma: "Don't do die, do also die." Yet, it can be just as bad if a person doesn't know how to die! The Hainanese say, *"Bo pard ti."* In Malay, the word is *mati*. Sometimes, *habis* (the end) is muttered instead.

There is a positive twist to the use of the word when evoking the *never say die* spirit. My colleague often breaks down into near despair but bounces back quickly with unflinching determination when handed a difficult assignment by the boss: *"Mati mati* also must do." In other words, he will literally work on it even if he were dying! Or, until he drops dead.

My mother has a euphemism for someone who dies or passes away: she says he has gone home. It is not all that unfamiliar a line; in many a Christian obituary, we come across the announcement that someone has been "called home to be with the Lord." A comforting thought, indeed. And a reminder too that we end where we begin: ashes to ashes, dust to dust.

120
THE HOLE OF OPPORTUNITIES

Two businessmen meet on the street and one says to the other: "Got any *lubang* or not?"

Lubang is Malay for *hole*.

It is amazing how we seek opportunities in holes, like treasure troves tucked away in the most unsuspected locations. Give a dog a bone and it will dig a hole in the garden to hide it. In this respect, we might do better were we tiny ants, squirrels, moles or mice and rats – talk about the rat race indeed!

Lubang can also mean connections or contacts that give one an entrée – as when a concerned parent seeks the assistance of some eminent person to admit his child into a good school. Imagine the holes of the rings in a chain!

And don't overlook that loophole which can offer opportunities in different ways. Caught in tight situations, we will want some escape route. Naturally, we look for a *lubang* as the way out. Interestingly, when someone *pecah lubang* (break a hole), he is said to have let the cat out of the bag!

121
CHOPE ME A PLACE

"Don't forget to *chope* a place for me!"

The closest English equivalent is *book, save* or *reserve*, but the local term connotes more than just placing an order for something, or sticking a *Sold* tag on an article, or hanging a *reserved* card on a chair. It is best understood in the context of an absence of an orderly system for designating items or places no longer available, and perhaps used with invigorating undertones of *kiasuism*.

In the sixties, when streetside Chinese wayangs were popular, people would tie chairs with handkerchiefs to *chope*

places or place mats and stools in preferred locations if no chairs were provided. The amazing thing was that everybody understood and respected the unwritten rules, and incidents of squabbles over territorial displacement were few and far between.

You can *chope* almost anything.

It is a useful word when you don't want to attend a wedding dinner and be seated among strangers or when you eye a piece of cake that is the only one of its kind left on the tray. One thing for sure, when speed is of the essence, it is much easier and faster to *chope* than reserve.

122
SO LECEH!

This is a colloquial Malay term popular among Malays and non-Malays, including foreigners who so very quickly assimilate everything Singaporean.

A Canadian who has lived in Singapore for a year surprised me when she complained it is "so *leceh*" travelling between Singapore and Toronto, making some five stops en route and having to change airlines and planes. Isn't there a faster and more convenient route, she asked. Fly Singapore Airlines, of course!

Leceh has indeed become a very useful, all-encompassing word. When it is troublesome to weed the garden blade by blade of some wild-growing plants, it is *so leceh*! When the boss wants you to rehash a 100-page document, it is *so leceh*! When you have to take a bus from Changi to Jurong just to collect a missing component of an electronic recorder you have just bought, it is *so leceh*! When you have to recopy a text that has been wiped off the face of your computer terminal because someone has accidentally pulled off the plug, it is *so leceh*! And if you have to dress up to the nines for a function when you feel more comfortable in T-shirt and jeans, it is *so leceh* indeed!

The Chinese have an equivalent, which is *sien*, often muttered with a sigh if not followed by a big yawn!

123
TAK PAKAI

An argument that is invalid is *tak pakai* – Malay for *cannot be used*. A fake coin is *tak pakai* and may lead you into trouble if you insist on using it knowingly. Conversely, you may ask whether your bus ticket is *pakai* or not for rides on the MRT.

Ever heard this story of two women, one wealthy and the other poor? The rich woman wears a zircon and passes it off as a diamond. Everyone is impressed by the size of the stone and its cut. The poor woman, on the other hand, wears a *real* diamond but everyone thinks it is an imitation stone. "No *pakai*" is what all of them say.

124
SUPERSTITIONS

We were visiting a colleague in hospital when I noticed someone missing in the party. Our colleague had just delivered a baby.

"Where's Jeanette?"

"She's not coming."

"Why not? She and Ivy are the best of friends."

"Because she's *pantang*."

In other words, Jeanette is the superstitious sort. Being *pantang*, she will not eat a baby's full-month (or *full moon* as some Chinese might prefer to call it) cake. She will not join a wake or attend a funeral. She will not invite anyone who is mourning to her home. And she will not step into a hospital unless it is she who is ill. Hence Jeanette's absence when we went to congratulate Ivy, never mind that it was good news that brought us there.

People who are *pantang* are wary about *black* and *white* clashing (figuratively), and that explains why some of them will shun clothes that combine those two shades. Do not dress in full black when visiting a *pantang* family. The edict of the *black/white superstition* propounds that happy and tragic events must be kept apart: a pregnant woman will avoid attending a wake or funeral, a person about to be married will not invite a friend who is mourning, and a son must marry within three months of his parent's death (if that happens) or wait three years.

Two happy events must not clash either. So if two good friends decide to marry at the same time, neither of them will invite the other to join in the celebrations. Because, according to Jeanette, it can be *shuay* (Hokkien for *bad luck*). And she will hasten to add, "Don't fool around with superstitions."

125
GO HOME

The genesis of this might be rooted in the Country Mouse and City Mouse fable.

Home may be home, sweet home, but *balik kampung* (Malay for *go back to the village*) is not really a friendly expression of farewell. It is usually uttered with contempt, dismissing someone by telling him to go back to where he belongs. And *kampung* is no idyllic Garden of Eden, but some place neglected by progress.

126
A BUMP ON THE HEAD

Exclaims the alarmed mother of a child who has taken a tumble from a chair: "Wah, such a big buah duku on your head! How come you fall down?"

Buah duku (the Chinese may pronounce it *baluku*) is the Malay name for a fruit with a thick, rubbery skin which is often used by mischievous boys as bullets for catapults. The sections of white flesh within are sweet and just a little tart.

The imagery is interesting. I like to think that it can be substituted with other fruits such as the *chiku* and *rambutan*. Probably not the *longan* (so named in Chinese as the dragon's eye), and even far less probably the *mata-kuching* (named in Malay the cat's eye because of its smaller size).

127
ALL'S FAIR IN WAR & LOVE

When you're driving and someone cuts into your path, he is said to *potong jalan*.

But that expression is more popularly used figuratively.

Remember *The Tennessee Waltz* and how one man loses his sweetheart to his best friend? That friend has *potong jalan*. A sad song, indeed, but all's fair in war and love, and may the best man win!

128
CHILD'S PLAY

I was sitting in the pew listening to the priest preaching his Sunday sermon, lampooning the laxity with which young couples treat the holy sacrament of marriage. "Today they marry," he lamented, visibly upset. "Tomorrow they divorce. What do they think they're doing? Playing *masak-masak?*"

Masak-masak is what little girls like playing. Dolls and a host of other toys are used, including little teapots, teacups, bowls, plates, spoons, forks, pots, pans, ladles, ovens, stoves, mock bottles of milk, packets of cereal, fruit, leaves, mud and almost anything that can be found in the house or garden. The play, of course, is imaginary.

In Malay, *masak* means *cook*. That – the domestic nature of the activities rather than the figurative use of the word – probably explains why *masak-masak* is a pastime for girls rather than boys, who may prefer more vigorous games such as *keledek, cateh,* and *hantam bola*. But when the priest mentioned *masak-masak*, there was no doubt that he included the men as well. It takes two hands to clap!

Glossary: Games That Boys Play
keledek: horseback riding. Participants throw stones from a distance to a line. Those whose stones land farthest away from the line will have to carry on their backs those whose stones are nearest the line. The rider will throw his stone while "on horseback" and challenge the bearer to hit it

with his stone. If the bearer misses, he will continue to bear the weight of the rider, trot towards the stones, pick them up and hand them to the rider who will then renew the challenge. This goes on until the bearer succeeds in hitting the rider's stone with his stone.

cateh: foot shuttle. A player lifts a shuttle made of feathers stuck to a rubber base. He kicks it up with his ankle or any part of the foot. The game may be varied with players passing the shuttle from one to another. The player who fails to catch it defaults.

hantam bola: ball hitting. This is a rough game that can be painful to the flesh. Whoever gets hold of the ball takes aim and hits another player with it.

129
KIAM SIAP & HUM SAP

Kiam siap is Hokkien and *hum sap* is Cantonese, and non-Hokkien or non-Cantonese speakers are apt to confuse them.

Don't be *kiam siap* and don't be *hum sap* are definitely not the same thing. Shylock falls into the former category (the stingy, miserly type) and many men with more than just an eye for pretty women qualify for the latter (the lecherous, lascivious kind). Both terms are interestingly salt-based.

One wonders how the venerable common salt has been given such rude treatment when the older Chinese man always says to his progeny that he has taken more salt than the youngster has consumed rice. (Kids of today who go for the salt in the ever popular french fries available at practically every fast food joint could well end up taking more salt than their master!)

A *hum sap* person (or *hum sap lo*) is really a *chico* man, who should not be mistaken for a salesman of Italian baby products. *Chico* is Hokkien for cheeky, lascivious or lecherous. And if that person of questionable repute is an old man, he is a *chico pek*.

130
A TIGER IN THE BUSH OR GOOD WINE NEEDS NO BUSH

If you don't know, don't *gasak buta* (guess blindly) or you will land in trouble. It is worse when you *goreng* (literally *fry* in Malay) or *sien* (Hokkien) or *bullshit*. Most people can easily detect a gasbag before long: it has to fart sometime. So wise is the person who may prefer to *buat bodoh* (pretend stupidity or ignorance), even if he knows more than others expect of him. He waits, like the silent tiger in the bush.

Or, shall we say too, good wine needs no bush?

131
AGAK AGAK

Agak agak is a very useful expression, particularly when you are dealing with numbers and do not know exactly how much something costs, its weight, its size or the time it was delivered to your office. But don't confuse this expression meaning *approximately* with seaweed jelly, which makes excellent party food. That is *agar agar*.

132
AS YOU LIKE IT

An angry mother rebukes her wayward son: "*Suka suka* you come. *Suka suka* you go. What do you think this house is? A hotel?"

Well, like it or not, the young man ought to know that even a hotel has its house rules.

Singapore Slips
and one from across the Causeway

133
BOY OR GIRL, MAKE A GUESS

When you travel in a bus, sometimes you just can't help eavesdropping. There is nothing like an interesting piece of news or conversation (albeit somebody else's) to revitalise you as you waste away in the heat. Travelling on the subway in New York, I was treated to raw drama – it was like living in a city overcrowded with actors. In Singapore, there is perhaps not so much drama, but your antenna can pick up some interesting quips.

I overheard, on an SBS bus, this exchange between two excitable women:

"Guess what? Mrs Tan has just got a baby."

"That's great news. Boy or girl?"

"Make a guess."

"Boy."

"Wrong! Make another guess."

"Girl."

"Right. How come you're so clever at guessing!"

Silly? Indeed, how often do we consciously listen to the stuff that spills from our own mouths?

134
SECOND CHANCE

Scene: Changi Beach.

Characters: A mother and her child.

Action: The child wobbles down the beach towards the sea, oblivious of the hazard of the rising tide.

The angry mother screams, "You listen to me and come

back here on the beach right now! Otherwise, when you drown, don't come back and cry to me, I won't pity you then."

Impact rating: High and immediate, like the rising tide. Message understood. The child heeds his mother's advice and comes running back to her.

135
DECEMBER 25 IS CHRISTMAS

I am always amused by a letter issued each year by the personnel department of a certain company inviting staff to apply for advance pay for the Christmas holiday. It begins: "This year, Christmas will fall on 25 December …"

It is like someone asking for the date of the New Year's Eve ball!

As far as I know, last year and the years before, Christmas came on 25 December. Maybe next year, as suggested by the personnel manager's note, it may not fall on 25 December. Someone should warn Santa.

136
HEARD ON RADIO

Programme 1

"The temperature will range between 29 degrees to a high of 32 degrees Celsius." A colleague of mine got so incensed by the consistent error that he called up the station. Since then it has been "between 29 and 32 degrees Celsius" or "from 29 to 32 degrees Celsius."

Programme 2

This was heard on the Breakfast Show of Radio One on 26 July 1991: "Can you repeat that again?"

Just say that again, Mr Disc Jockey.

Programme 3

"Time by Northwest Airlines is 5.54 p.m. Over in Honolulu, it's 11.54 last evening." (Date of broadcast: 19 August 1994)

Who says we cannot travel back in time? Or into the future? I can imagine the disc jockey in Honolulu announcing, "Over in Singapore, it's 5.54 tomorrow evening."

137
REASON IN MADNESS

This is the story of a VIP who visits some hospitals in Singapore as part of an official programme to induct him into the Health Ministry.

First Stop: General Hospital. The VIP is shown the operating theatre and told that local anaesthetic is administered for the patients. He applauds: "Good, very good, we must promote the use of local products."

Second Stop: Kandang Kerbau Hospital. As they enter a ward marked *Labour*, the VIP hesitates and steps back, saying: "If this belongs to the Ministry of Labour, I don't want to interfere."

Third Stop: Woodbridge Hospital. The VIP is warned that he will see the inmates doing strange things. He is advised to humour the inmates and pretend he understands what they are doing, however abnormally they act. So when the VIP chances upon a man sitting in the middle of a concrete yard with a fishing rod in his hand, he says to the inmate, "So, I see, you're fishing." The inmate barks in reply, "You *gila*, ah, here no water how can you fish?"

Gila is Malay for *mad*. The Chinese would have said *seow*. The *New Paper* (14 July 1994) reported on the hosts of *Asia Bagus*, a TV variety show, as follows: "Tomoko is the pretty Japanese deejay who speaks sedate American English while her co-hosts Najip Ali and Moses Lim tease her with their Singlish and *gila* (crazy) behaviour." Other words are similarly used, and how acrimonious they are depends on the circumstances in which they are used; these words include *suku* (a quarter) and *ting tong*.

Is there reason in madness? Perhaps only the madman knows!

138
A TIME TO KILL

Little children display an inimitable zest for drama that is clearly visible in their movements and in the things they utter.

Two little imps are playing cowboys with toy guns. One of them screams: "Bang! Bang! Kill him die! Kill him die!" One wonders if it is the literal translation of the Hokkien *pak see*, which is *beat to death*. Anyway, the other child collapses, muttering as he groans and puts a hand to an imaginary wound on his chest, "I die already."

139
IN BLOCK CAPITALS

This advertisement, which appeared in the *Straits Times*, was inserted on behalf of a training school in England, inviting readers to take up a home-study Diploma in Business English course. It welcomed applicants to "write now, giving your name and address in BLOCK CAPITALS."

Are there small capitals, I wonder? And I don't mean Washington, D.C.

140
THE CENTRE

Why do so many people say the *central core*? Can the core be anywhere else but in the centre, or be anything but central?

It's like breaking a bar of chocolate into halves and asking which is the bigger half. It is, however, different when a man refers to his wife as the better half.

141
TWO THINGS YOU SHOULD NOT DO

In public places, you see notices such as "Do not eat and drink in the auditorium" and "Do not swim and fish in the pond." They usually spell out clearly two things you cannot do; in the two given examples, these are "do not eat in the auditorium and do not drink in the auditorium", and "do not swim in the pond and do not fish in the pond."

I get a little queasy when I stumble upon this caption to a story: "Do not speed and drive with caution during bad weather." The notice spells out two things that you should not do during bad weather: *do not speed* and *do not drive with caution*. A simple rewording would unscramble the message: *"Do not speed during bad weather. Drive with caution."*

It is a serious message, and whoever issues it ought to get it right the first time round.

142
FIRST COME FIRST SERVED

I confess to getting a little agitated when people put up notices that say "first come first serve". It is, rightly, "first come first *served*."

I received a letter from a reputable university that reads as follows: "Applications will close on 15 August 1994. However, as the number of students [shouldn't it be *places*?] is limited, we will appreciate your early application. Successful application [sic] will be admitted on a *first-come-first-serve* basis."

The expression is perhaps best understood when we dissect it into two parts: *the first to come* and *the first to be served*. The person who is the first to arrive does not serve; he gets served – and served first – instead. Of course, the server must be there first, but the rule does not apply to him.

And if it is a self-serve facility, we might say that the early bird catches the worm.

143
COME & GO

I brought my children to a playground and ended up collecting a list of amusing *come and go* expressions:

"I tell you to take him *go there*."

"Do you want to bring your child *come here*?"

"Take *come here* my things, won't you?"

"Bring him *go there* and play."

"I say, why did you push him *go there* on the sand?"

Familiar? Well, just let them go as they come. We know well enough that it is *come here* and *go there*. But, on reflection, I hesitate: do we really?

144
PLAY CHEAT

We play fair and dirty, play fast and loose, play hard to get, play safe and play ball with someone, but I'm not sure about the Singaporean concoction of *play cheat*.

145
NEITHER A BORROWER
NOR A LENDER BE

Neither a borrower nor a lender be. That probably explains why so many Singaporeans confuse the words *borrow* (to take from someone) and *lend* (to give).

Another confusion often heard has to do with the word *owe*. Some tongues wag it like *own*. I like to think that it is my poor hearing. But if you *owe* someone some money, it is very unlikely that you will *own* him.

I DIDN'T STEAL IT, I LEND IT FROM HIM SIR

14 DAYS FOR THEFT; AND ONE MONTH FOR BAD ENGLISH!

TRIGG

146
TOO MUCH, TOO LITTLE; TOO MANY, TOO FEW

Too *much* sauce and too *little* noodles, but too *many* people and too *few* chairs. *Many* (men) are called, but *few* are chosen. Why cry over a love lost when (figuratively) there are *many* fish in the ocean? The Ancient Mariner will recall that although there was so *much* water around him and his dead mates, there was not a drop to drink. My hairstylist tells me I have *not much* or *little* hair left on my head. He knows *many* people but has *little* knowledge of their private lives. Our teachers will warn parents that too *much* play and too *little* work will not make their children clever. Remember the Dionne Warwick song about what the world needs badly? Well, there can never be too *much* love and we pray that there will be as *little* hate as possible.

We use *many* and *few* when we can count the items, and *much* and *little* when we cannot easily identify the subjects by numbers.

With qualifiers, the job becomes easier. Too *much* cake but *many* pieces of cake. Too *much* barley but *many* bowls of barley. Too *much* sand but *many* grains of sand. Too *little* hair but *few* strands of hair. Too *little* work but a *few* assignments to complete. Too *little* money but a *few* dollars left in the pocket.

According to Confucius, it is wise not to have too much or too little of something; always strike the golden mean.

147
WHEN IT IS TOO MUCH

This advice came from a colleague when he learnt that I had a sore throat: "Don't eat durian *too much*."

Well, considering the price of the fruit (the *bao jia* or guaranteed type), one seldom gets to eat *too much* durian!

148
A MATTER OF LOCATION

Scene: A supermarket.

Characters: A lost customer and a sales assistant.

Action: The customer walks up and down the aisles, looking confused and exasperated. He is unable to locate an item. He approaches the sales assistant for help.

The sales assistant replies: "Sorry, I'm not salesgirl in here." Then she struts away.

The customer is annoyed. He notes that the sales assistant is uniformed like other sales personnel in that store, so there's no mistake about her working in the store. Later, he finds her in another section of the store and she steps up to him, "Sir, can I help you? I'm salesgirl in HERE."

Only then does he realise what she means.

149
A MATTER OF DEGREE

Your child spoke perfect English until she went to school and now she comes home saying, "good, gooder, goodest" because the other children say so and the teacher does not correct them. What do you do then?

This is not a rarity or an exaggeration. A good number of the people out there coin their own comparatives and superlatives when they aren't sure. And an equally good number of people like double emphases in expressions such as *more heavier*, *more better* and *more rounder*. Others who don't like comparatives are content with *more good*, *more sad* and *more pretty*. And, of course, there are the overzealous lot who swear by *most happiest*, *most cleverest* and *most highest*.

It's a matter of degree, you might say.

150
PERFECTION PAR EXCELLENCE

Singaporeans love superlatives, and this penchant is promulgated by the media. Sports achievers, for example, are praised sky high as though they had reached the pinnacle of their career and had no room left for improvement. The inconsistent performance of some of them makes one wonder whether we have done more harm than good being so free and indiscriminate in our praise.

Perfect is a favourite word among us, but to say *very perfect* is stretching the accolade a little too far. We tend to use the adverb *very* rather loosely for emphasis, as in "Your suggestion is *very ideal*" or "The moon is *very round* tonight." If it is perfect, it is the best. If it is ideal, no other can be better. And nothing can be more round than round, not even *perfectly round*. It seems to be a case of too much perfection or a precision so precise it becomes too good to be true!

And if that's not good enough, a service company claiming to be world class publicly announces that it aims to be "above the rest, better than the best."

151
SEEING DOUBLE

Aren't you tired of people asking for your IC card number? (*IC* equals *identity card*, therefore *IC card number* equals *identity card card number*).

Do people tell you that they're working on the PC computer? (*PC* equals *personal computer*, therefore PC computer equals …).

But what's so wrong about those when one of the top banks here, the Development Bank of Singapore, is the DBS Bank?

152
USING THE TELEPHONE

I received this letter from a business associate: "Kindly refer to our *telephonic* conversation …"

We did have a conversation using the telephone. But a *telephonic* conversation? Come to think of it, why not when it is an electronic typewriter, a stereophonic recording or a telescopic view? It appears so logical until you remember that it is a *telephone* directory, a *telephone* booth and a *telephone* exchange. Since the directory, booth and exchange are not *telephonic*, by the same token a conversation conducted via telephone cables is not! We simply had a *telephone conversation* as different from a tete-a-tete at a coffee-house. Some people now say *tele*-conversation.

153
HELLO, CAN I HELP?

I called up a reputable organisation and a sweet voice responded, "Hello, what can I help you?"

She stumped me momentarily and I forgot *what* it was I wanted. I wasn't sure anyway *what* she could do to help me then. Or *how* she could help me. But you can be sure that it wasn't her voice, sweet as it was, that had me dumbfounded.

154
PAIN IS PAINFUL

Too many people are using *pain* instead of *painful* as an adjective. When someone gets hurt, his sympathisers will ask, "Pain or not?" And the reply? "Not pain."

One of the girls at our office told us about her visit to the dentist. She complained he kept asking her "pain or not?" (and other questions) when all she could say with his hands in her mouth was a blabbering "ahhh ..." And when she started squirming and tightening up all the muscles in her body, he would say quickly, "No pain, no pain." It was painful! But she couldn't get the message across.

Indeed, why do dentists have to ask their patients questions when they know very well their helpless victims in the swivelling chairs cannot utter an intelligible word in reply?

Whatever it is, *pain* must be *painful*!

155
THE COOKER COOKS

This slipped from the mouth of an undergraduate who invited some classmates home to dinner: "My mother is a good cooker."

Well, if someone who swims is a swimmer and someone who plays the drums is a drummer, someone who cooks must be a cooker.

156
WIN, LOSE OR DRAW

It is Singaporean to want to win in almost any contest or game. It is, after all, the *kiasu* syndrome! At children's colouring competitions, you see parents helping their children with the pencils. "We must *win* them (rivals)," they urge.

We *win* games and we *win* people over, but we don't *win* our rivals or opponents. We beat them instead by fair means or foul.

Conversely, we can convey quite a different meaning if we say "we must not *lose* them (rivals)". If we lose a game, we are beaten or defeated by our rivals. Therefore if we want to win, we cannot afford to *lose* to our opponents. But we wouldn't mind losing them along the way, would we?

Happy are those who win, and sad those who lose. And there are always the cautious few who prefer *no win, no lose*.

Conquer is sometimes mistaken for *win*. Alexander the Great, Attila the Hun, Kublai Khan and Napoleon Bonaparte fought many wars, but they didn't conquer wars; they conquered territories and the enemies instead, and they won many wars.

Another error commonly detected in print is the confusion between *lose* and *loose*. The *Straits Times* of 31 October 1985 reported that "Trade and Industry Minister Dr Tony Tan last night had a message for businessmen: Keep investing and do not *loose* confidence because of the economic downturn." Call it a typographical error, if you will, in this case, but there are others who just cannot see the visible meaning of the *oo* in *loose* to mean not tight.

157
FOR WHOM THE BELLS TOLL

More than a thousand couples in Singapore were married on 14 February 1995 because St Valentine's Day coincided with *Yuan Xiao Jie*, the 15th day of the Lunar New Year. This auspicious day in the Chinese calendar may be said to be the equivalent of the traditional, western St Valentine's Day. On this day, young maidens in ancient China were said to throw oranges in streams to catch their match – those young men who were quick to pick up the fruits of their hearts!

The *Straits Times* on 15 February reported the bumper crop of marriages under the headline, "Wedding bells toll – and toll and toll". One concerned parent apparently called up

Times House and protested against the use of the word *toll*. When I was told this, I consulted my dictionaries. Yes, bells toll, but the slow, regular strokes are usually used for a death or funeral. For weddings, we prefer to hear bells *peal* or *chime* or simply *ring*. You may recall that jolly song from *My Fair Lady* that goes, "I'm getting married in the morning. Ding dong the bells are gonna chime ..."

Interestingly, the *Straits Times* carried a story three days later about a wedding couple who beat up a drunken Romanian priest at the altar because he read out a funeral oration during their wedding ceremony. That happened in Bucharest.

158
NO SWIMMING ALLOWED

This one is not a Singapore slip but one from across the Causeway, reproduced from a sign at the Kota Tinggi Waterfall, which was once a popular getaway picnic spot for Singaporeans. At the main pool, the sign reads: "Anyone including children who cannot swim are advised to swim at the pools below."

Who really are the people who should be swimming at the pools below, apart from *anyone including children who cannot swim*? And if they cannot swim, how can they swim at the pools below?

My friend and I who visited Kota Tinggi many years ago didn't go there to swim. For the benefit of swimmers and non-swimmers, adults and children, I hope the old sign has been replaced by one that is less ambiguous.

Last Word

159
LAST WORD: MATE

Mate has to be the last entry for my book.

An engineer issues this exhortation to the staff working at the airport: "When the aircraft engine is running, the operator will not be allowed to mate the aerobridge with the aircraft …" An interesting and boldly vivid use of the word *mate* to mean *join* or *dock*, I thought. For those who don't know, an *aerobridge*, a walkway that operates like a drawbridge, is connected to an aircraft for the embarkation or disembarkation of passengers.

I used to hear how we *marry* things – figuratively, that is. Now we've gone a step ahead to *mate* them!

When we start mating nuts and bolts, a window and its hinges, the stove and a gas cylinder, etc., my Australian friends, who have an irresistible fondness for that word, might well ask, *What's next, mate?*

THE AUTHOR

David Leo has published two collections of short stories, a book of poetry and a novella. Both collections of short stories have won prizes.

Born in Singapore, his romance with the English language started at a very young age when he dabbled in rhymes. He graduated with an Honours degree in English from the University of Singapore and went on to become a teacher by choice for some years. Some of the material for the book came from those engaging schooldays. He went about the compilation no differently from someone collecting stamps or matchboxes.

Mr Leo swims, dreams and enjoys cryptic crosswords after a hard day's work at the office.